The Earliest Church

The Earliest Church

Rev. William P. Sampson, SJ

Rev. James P. M. Walsh, SJ, ed.

Washington, DC

New Academia Publishing, 2016

Printed in the United States of America

Library of Congress Control Number: 2016932117
ISBN 978-0-9966484-6-2 paperback (alk. paper)

New Academia Publishing
4401-A Connecticut Ave., N W #236 - Washington, DC 20008
info@newacademia.com - www.newacademia.com

Contents

Editors' Notes

William Sampson, a Jesuit priest, died in his seventy-second year after three decades of giving retreats, both directed and preached, in the United States and in India. He carried on a long correspondence with a wide variety of persons—very often Catholic Sisters and others who had made retreats under his direction—and at a certain point drew together much of what he had written in letters and articles into a small book called *The Coming of Consolation: How God Gets Through to Us.*

The book was written longhand. I typed it for him and then set about trying to find a publisher for it. From then on Bill referred to me as "my editor."

He eventually learned how to use a computer but we continued to collaborate on his writing projects, notably *Meeting Jesus.*

When he died he had finished one more book, a companion volume to *Meeting Jesus* that is to it as St. Luke's *Acts of the Apostles* is to Luke's *Gospel.* The final text was on a floppy disk, which nestled in a desk drawer in my office for almost a decade. A sabbatical year afforded me the time to retrieve it, bring it up to date technologically, and go to work tracking down and double-checking references, formatting material of different sorts, and replacing all the Scriptural quotations with the translation found in the newly published *New American Bible,* Revised Edition (NABRE).

It was a privilege to do this editorial work on my friend's manuscript. I am sorry I took so long getting to it.

J.P.M. Walsh, SJ
Associate Professor
Department of Theology
Georgetown University

In 2013 Rev. James Walsh, SJ (1937-2015), brought two manuscripts to my Georgetown office. One was his own book *Seeing Things: How Your Imagination Shapes You and Your World*, published by the Georgetown University Office of the President in time for Christmas 2015. The other manuscript was this book, written by his late friend Father William P. Sampson, SJ (1928-2000), for whom Father Walsh acted as literary executor. Whenever Father Walsh discussed publishing either book, he always put Father Sampson's ahead of his own. It was clear that he cared more for its future than for that of his own work. The Office of the President is now bringing out Father Sampson's book in time for Easter 2016, fulfilling Father Walsh's generous and spiritual concern that Father Sampson's lovely book be available to readers. Thank you to Dr. Anna Lawton and the New Academia editorial board for our shared work on these books, to Toby Terrar and the Maryland Province of the Society of Jesus for author photos, and to Dr. John Glavin for again advising on these thoughts.

Carole Sargent, PhD, Director
Office of Scholarly Publications
Georgetown University

About the Author

The author in 2000, and in 1963 at Gonzaga College High School in Washington, DC.

William P. Sampson (1928-2000) was a Jesuit priest who followed a decade of teaching high school with thirty years of work giving retreats. His insights into the Spiritual Exercises of St. Ignatius of Loyola, and his masterly guidance of hundreds of nuns, priests, and lay persons on Ignatian retreats, greatly influenced many religious congregations in the post-Vatican II era. His previous writings include *The Coming of Consolation: How God Gets Through to Us*, and *Meeting Jesus*.

The Earliest Church

Introduction

Beginnings hold a fascination for us. When we encounter something phenomenal, we are drawn to its beginnings—how did it start? What was the moment when it first appeared?

The Protestant movement, for example. It spread so rapidly through sixteenth-century Europe. It began with a single priest. So we try to find out all we can about him: what were the influences on him. Especially important is that moment and that experience before which he was not yet a Protestant, and after which he was. That moment is studied. It's the kernel, the fundamental, the ultimate ground of all that follows.

We study its development. We watch how, step by step, this seed grew into what we know today. Those early years, when so many options were still open, fascinate us. How come it went this way and not that?

Only when we get some clues as to what happened then can we relive the experience of that priest, Martin Luther. Otherwise we are limited to reading it all backward and when we do that, everything that happened has a certain inevitability about it. But for those who lived it, it was far from inevitable that it would develop the way it did. At the time it was happening, it seemed so open-ended, so filled with possibilities, and so in need of decisions.

Like Robert Frost's narrator in his poem "The Road Not Taken," when we look backward we have it all figured out. Here's the path I took and here were the consequences, and none of this would have happened had I gone down the other path. It's so pat. It's missing a crucial ingredient. It isn't the way it was. To understand it better, we have to find out what it was like for those in the middle of it.

Recently I saw a televised production of Charles Dickens' *A Tale of Two Cities*. As I watched, I was sorry I already knew the ending. How I wished that I had never read it before. An edge was gone that would have made such a difference in my enjoyment. In Dickens' day the work appeared a few chapters at a time in a monthly magazine. Nobody knew what was going to happen to Darnay. They lived through it with him.

In a previous book, *Meeting Jesus,* I tried to imagine Jesus' life as he experienced it, from within, in the dark about the future, making one decision at a time. In this book I would like to do the same for the years just after the death and resurrection of Jesus.

What was it like for those who lived the first years of Christianity? What do we know about their scene? Can we get into the options that they faced, and the choices that they made and the choices that they rejected? Can we remove the weight of inevitability that keeps us from reliving their lives, from imagining ourselves back there, in the dark about the future? Can we relive their decisions?

Any effort along this line comes up against a fact about this period of history that has well been stated by one of the scholars of Hellenistic religion, A. Deissmann: "The origin of the cult of Christ (and that means, of christology) is the secret of the earliest Palestinian community."[1]

We simply do not have the data to re-create with certainty what the actual sequence of events in those earliest years was.

However, this does not leave us without anything to say about those years, as thousands of articles and books testify. But it does mean that we are operating in a world of probabilities, plausibilities, and impossibilities. Just as when physicists study the origin of the universe, the lack of hard data does not rule out endless speculating by the finest scientific minds, so, too, those interested in Christian origins are constantly discussing and trying to distinguish the probable from the impossible, the plausible, and the unlikely.

What I offer here is a projection, one possible scenario of what might have happened in those earliest years. I select what I consider the most plausible scenario. As Otto Betz wrote in *What Do We Know About Jesus?* "The Gospels force us to make our own picture of Jesus, one which will do justice both to [the testimony of the four

Gospels] and to our own restless urge for truth."[2] So, too, in the New Testament, The Acts of the Apostles and especially the Letters of Paul force us to make our own picture of the earliest Church.

We are doing what the author of Acts tried to do for his audience: give them some indication of how it must have been to be alive and in the middle of it all during those first years.

My own interest was aroused by a work of Larry Hurtado, *One God, One Lord*, a study of early Christian devotion.[3] This led me to the many writings of Martin Hengel of Tübingen in which he studies the earliest years of Christianity. His work has been built upon by so many others.

Hengel states his central concern well in the opening paragraph of his *The Son of God*:

> At the feast of the Passover in the year 30, in Jerusalem, a Galilean Jew was nailed to the cross for claiming to be Messiah. About twenty-five years later, the former Pharisee Paul quotes a hymn about this crucified man in a letter which he writes to one of the communities of the messianic sect which he has founded in the Roman colony of Philippi... The discrepancy between the shameful death of a Jewish state criminal and the confession that depicts this executed man as a pre-existent divine figure who becomes man and humbles himself to a slave's death is, as far as I can see, without analogy in the ancient world.[4]

That "discrepancy" between the events of AD 30 and the creation of the hymn contained in Paul's letter provides me with the time period I will focus on, the very earliest Church.

It was during that brief period that the earliest Palestinian community became involved in the cult of Christ. It is a time wrapped in darkness for us. There is not the light that would be produced by letters or autobiographies, or financial statements, or odds and ends written by those who were there.

We enter a dark room. We must pause and let our eyes get used to the darkness. What we will see are shadows, vague, incomplete forms, a glint here and there. "What is that form near the window?" "Is it a computer?" That's a possibility. "Maybe it's a gas heater." "No. It's too narrow."

Into the darkness we project possibilities. We try them out. That's what I am doing here, projecting a possibility. For these earliest years that's all we can do, produce scenarios of what might have happened. Events did take place. People did make decisions. These decisions did lead them on to strange paths. Changes did occur. By the time the lights go on, much has already happened.

Here is one of the common scenarios:

> A band of disciples totally disheartened by the Passover events flees to Galilee. There they gradually become convinced that Jesus' death could not have been the end of such a spectacularly good life. The goodness they had seen in him could not have been buried in his tomb. Such a finale would mean that God was totally indifferent to human goodness. The Jesus-Event must be continuing in a triumphant mode. He must be still existing. In his new mode of existence, Jesus must have received a vindication from God. In a way hidden from the world, his story has continued and a new final chapter has been written in the heavens. Jesus is still alive!
>
> As the days pass they attend their synagogues and reflect on the nature of this new life of Jesus. Certain texts of the Scripture become clues to the particulars of Jesus' new life. He is seen as being the enthroned one, the power above all powers, the one to be prayed to and sung about.
>
> But they are still believers in Yahweh. There is only the one God. They are still devout Jews, monotheists, members of the synagogue, and when they come to Jerusalem, they worship in the Temple.
>
> After a time, they begin to admit pagans into their sect. This creates conflict with the religious leaders, and more importantly opens the Church to influences very alien to Judaism. The pagans have been converted from religions which revered many gods in the heavens. Divinity was shared by a crowd of personalities.
>
> When the converts from paganism begin to preach the good news to their fellow pagans, they naturally explain Jesus by translating him into their way of speaking about the divine. There is no way that they can deny to him divinity

> when it is the boast of so many lesser figures. These converts have none of the sensitivity of the Jews toward monotheism. It is in their circles that Jesus is spoken of as divine, and the Church is drawn toward the trinitarian faith that will dominate its history. It is among them that Jesus becomes the divine Son, true God of true God. Most of the writers of the New Testament come under their influence. They turn a Jewish sect into a totally new religion.

With many variations in detail, of course, this is a common scenario held by people over the last century.

But... did it happen this way? Who knows? We are in an area where guessing is inevitable.

For many Christians this scenario is impossible to believe. They see it as an invitation to stop believing. They are disturbed when they are told by some of the experts that this is the only possible way any reasonable person could read the events. They are tempted to give up believing—or to give up on reasoning.

But there are other scenarios that can be written. The one I will spell out in this book will be much more supportive of the traditional faith of Christians. Its plausibility will be indicated by the scholars who think along these lines, people whose expertise is honored throughout the field of scriptural scholarship even by those who disagree with their particular suggestions.

To the degree that the scenario presented here is likely, it will be useful. Where it is unlikely, may it stimulate others to produce better ones.

1

The Early Decisions

One of the first decisions the disciples make is to leave Galilee and return to Jerusalem for the great Festival of Weeks. They could have crept away, speechless from shame, and lived a life of prayer and penance, perhaps in Galilee, awaiting the return of Jesus. Like the Qumran community they could have gone into the desert and lived quiet lives of preparation for the great day.

But the Apostles do something quite different. They do not withdraw, though they are tempted along that path. Instead they decide to return to Jerusalem.

This decision is not reached after many months or years of reflection. No, within seven weeks they are back on the road heading for Jerusalem, back into that world where they are strangers and nobodies. In the time left before the return of Jesus, they leave their cozy and peaceful home base around the lake, their familiar surroundings where they know every nook and cranny. They walk back into the urban scene where they come across as country bumpkins, people who speak with an upcountry accent, backwoodsmen.

Looking back from where we are it can be hard to grasp how strange that decision was. It is easy from our retrospective view to see very little choosing in their return to Jerusalem so soon after the catastrophic events of the Passover feast. But to those involved, it was not at all an inevitable choice. They were spectacular failures in their own eyes. They were not likely candidates for any further missions. The best thing they could do now was to live apart and prepare peacefully and prayerfully for the end. But they decide otherwise.

Had they chosen to stay in Galilee, the story of the Church would have been very different. Perhaps we would never have heard of them.

Why did they decide to go back? What made them return to the hubbub of Jerusalem? They became convinced that they had a mission to accomplish. A sense of being-sent had come upon the group as a result of the appearances of Jesus, and the coming of the Spirit. They have been given a task. It is a very limited task: the good news is to be preached to the chosen people. A last chance is to be offered to the Jews before the end comes on.

So the earliest disciples do not decide to go the way of the separatist community of Qumran. They leave the lake country and head back down the Jordan valley, and take the road up from Jericho to Jerusalem. They walk into the Temple and preach to the people: "The end has come; here is the last chance for you; there is still time to be saved."

On their way back along the roads to Jerusalem they had passed again all the familiar sights. It is the third time they have made this journey in the last few months. It is also likely to be the last time. The end will not be long in coming. Their preaching will probably prove just as useless as was Jesus' preaching. But it is God's special favor to the chosen people, a final opportunity.

This then is the first thing to be noticed about the earliest disciples: they chose to return to Jerusalem. It is not an obvious decision, and it will have an enormous effect, of course, on the development of the Church.

The second decision they made would have appeared to them a very minor one, involving a new practice. At supper, they have one of the Apostles recall some of the words Jesus had used at the supper he had eaten with them just before his death. They remember Jesus telling them to do it. But he had told them to do many things, like washing each other's feet, and they did not feel obliged to follow them literally. But the command to repeat the words and gestures that he had used at that supper, this they decide to follow literally.

It is a small but crucial decision, and it will have immense consequences in the coming months. It will shape the community's future as nothing else. At the supper, in the evening, toward the beginning of the meal, there is a pause and one of the Apostles recalls the very words Jesus used and breaks some bread and passes it around the table as Jesus had done. Then, toward the end of the meal, he takes a cup of wine and repeats the words as best as he remembers them, and the cup passes from hand to hand as each one drinks. It is very brief. It is simply an interruption of the meal.

What if they had decided—consciously or unconsciously—to celebrate the Last Supper *only* as part of their annual Passover? The Eucharist would then occur as an annual memorial of the real meaning of Passover. Though they did not decide to do that, it would not have been an unlikely choice. Jesus had added those few words to an already developed ritual, and that ritual-setting was a help to explain the meaning of his brief additions.

Didn't repeating Jesus' words apart from the Passover setting prove to be somewhat awkward? What if Jesus had chosen the paschal lamb's flesh to symbolize his body? But he chose the bread. Did that make it easy for them to enter upon a pattern of using the Eucharistic ritual frequently?

In retrospect it is very easy to miss the options that were available to the disciples. It can appear that they had no choice but to do what Jesus had clearly planned for them. But the path they took was chosen by them from among many paths they might have gone down.

This then is the second decision they made within those first seven weeks. The Apostles bring with them on their mission to Jerusalem this practice of doing again and saying again what Jesus had so recently done and said at that supper, and what he had told them to do and say. It is a very small part of their day. It is only a small part of their supper. But it is quite different from what their suppers had been before. It is also different from what suppers are like elsewhere in Jerusalem.

The next two decisions are made unconsciously. They do *not* decide to change certain practices. For what is most striking about the group is not how they differ from other Jews but how similar they are. Two things that they do not change are most surprising. The first: they go to the Temple each day and engage in the Temple rituals just as they had always done. Peter takes two doves to the priest to be sacrificed. It never enters his head not to do it. Nothing that they have experienced makes them think that this is inappropriate, or a waste of time. They see themselves as the same devout Jews that they were before the death of Jesus. The Temple ritual is still as meaningful as ever. The sacrifices and the songs, the psalms and the prayers still touch their hearts. They participate in the service without questions. The coming of the new heavens and the new earth are but a completion of what they are already sharing in when they join in the Temple worship. The end is near but it will bring with it a new and more glorious Temple. They feel at home among the crowd of worshippers.

Don't they realize that they are Christians? That the Temple and its holocausts are at an end? That Jesus is the new Temple? That these sacrifices have lost all their meaning now?

How odd that after the Resurrection appearances, the followers of Jesus—the Earliest Church—go to the Temple each day, and pray to God with the priests.

But this confusion persisted among Christians for centuries. One strange instance occurred almost three hundred years after the Resurrection, in Antioch. Some Christians would attend the synagogue on the Sabbath and on the high holy days. John Chrysostom commented: "Many among us keep the Sabbath." They joined in the celebration of Yom Kippur, fasting as the Jews did. They erected huts for the festival of Sukkoth. As Robert Wilken in his study on Chrysostom states:

> These Christians who participated in Jewish rites and observed Jewish law were not marginal renegades who came to church only infrequently. From John's comments, they appear to be regular members of his congregation who thought they could remain members of the Church while observing Jewish rites and customs. In their minds, there was no contradiction between going to the synagogue on Saturday to hear the reading of the Law and coming to Church on Sunday to participate in the Eucharist. They want, says John, to have fellowship with the Jews and 'fellowship at the holy table sharing the precious blood.'[5]

So, too, the early disciples did not even think of not going to the Temple once they were back in Jerusalem.

Neither do the disciples stop going to the synagogue services. In the past, whenever they had come to Jerusalem they would on the Sabbath go to one of the synagogues in town. Now, they continue to do so. They do not experience any sense that these services have been rendered meaningless. Even though they are mixing with people who do not believe in Jesus, still they join in their prayers, they listen with them during the readings, they listen while the rabbi explains the text. That the rabbi is not a believer in Jesus is not important. They still feel that they share a common faith with him. They are all devout Jews. These are still the chosen people. What is coming will only bring this faith to a fullness of perfection.

These patterns of Temple worship and attendance at the synagogue services have important consequences. It means that they keep on hearing the Scripture read, the Law and the Prophets. It is going to be different from listening to the Law and the Prophets before. The disciples are no longer the same, and the texts will take on, in some cases, a strikingly different meaning.

We have noted how the decision not to live quietly in Galilee affected the future of the Church. Had they stayed near the lake, there would have been little challenge to their simple, undeveloped, relatively formless faith.

But what would have been the outcome had they separated immediately from Temple and synagogue—if that can even be imagined? The evolution would have taken a path where Scripture would have played a much less important role. But because they kept on with Temple and synagogue, hearing the texts of Scripture soon became part of a dialogue they are having with the Jerusalem Jews. Sometimes a question that a listener asks during the Temple preaching—often in a non-hostile way—is answered by a Scripture text they hear at the services later that day. This dialogue with their hearers is the context of their listening to the reading of Scripture. There are moments when a text leaps out at them as the precise answer to one of the questions.

Since they see themselves as devout Temple worshippers, they are stimulated intensely by Scripture. The Earliest Church will live and grow within Judaism. The Apostles will search the Scriptures for answers to their questions and for confirmation of their faith in Jesus.

This was the world of the Earliest Church. Temple worship and preaching to the people, a remembering at the supper, and the synagogue service, nothing that sharply distinguishes them from a typical Jewish sect. They are awaiting the return of Jesus in glory, and the end of the world, the coming of a new heaven and a new earth. This pattern could have gone on indefinitely, had it not been for unexpected developments. Two surprises were to radically change the path the Church was taking, and to produce a Church all but unrecognizable to the first followers.

2

Two Surprises

On their return to Jerusalem the disciples see once again familiar places which reawaken memories of the catastrophic Passover. The Roman soldiers here and there remind them of the great power of the Empire. The crowds of people bring back pictures of the hostility of that day, and how they had been screaming for Jesus to die. The priests in the Temple and the Pharisees are unpleasant reminders also.

The disciples go into the Temple areas to preach. It is then they encounter their first surprise: people actually listen! Instead of the violent hostility that was experienced just seven weeks before, they find people listening to them, asking them questions, getting interested. The Apostles are amazed.

The crowds in Jerusalem are immense. It is the Feast of Weeks, the first large gathering of the pilgrims since the Passover festival. The Apostles who had performed so shabbily during the Passover, filled with fear, are now quite boldly standing up before strangers in the Temple courts—just the way Jesus had—and not all the people are turning away. Some come to their synagogue services to hear more. And some finally join them completely, and are invited to the suppers.

It is a cause of great joy among the disciples. Here, in this alien world with its urbane culture, people are touched by their word. Of course, some of the better classes had been attracted by Jesus, but he was a most effective speaker. That was different. Now, it is their own voices that are being heard.

But there is a much greater surprise in store for them, and it also occurs in the first few weeks.

One morning, a week after their return to Jerusalem, Peter stands up in the Court of the Men and begins to preach. The disciples are gathered near him. People draw near. Some are familiar faces, people whom the disciples recognize for they had been frequently among the crowds that listened to Jesus preach.

The passersby are curious. They come up to the fringe of the crowd and ask those on the edge what's going on. Quite a few stay to listen. Two well-dressed men approach, drawn by Peter's fire. They ask one of the listeners, "Do you speak Greek?" "Very little." The two look on in curiosity. One of them sees Philip standing off to one side, and he brings the other man with him, weaving through the crowd to where Philip is standing.

Once Philip sees him coming, he remembers him well. They had met just a few months before in this same Temple, not far from this very spot. It had been evening and Jesus had just finished preaching. The crowd of listeners was slowly breaking up and the disciples were getting ready to walk to Bethany. Suddenly a group of rather wealthy people came toward Philip, and this man now approaching him had been the spokesperson. His name was Stephen. They were Jews who spoke Greek, not Aramaic. Many of them could not understand Jesus' words but there were a few in the group who knew some Aramaic, and they had been impressed by Jesus. Now they wanted to meet him personally. Someone had pointed out Philip to them as a disciple who spoke Greek.

That evening weeks before, Philip had taken them to Andrew for he also knew Greek, and they brought these men to Jesus (John 12:20). Now as Peter continues to preach to the growing crowd, Stephen and his friend, Nicolaus, introduce themselves to Philip. They ask to be caught up on the events. So Philip tells them the good news, in Greek. It is the first time that the gospel of the Risen One has been spoken in Greek! The two friends hear it with delight. They had been delighted by Jesus' words, and stunned at his execution. As Philip speaks, their old enthusiasm comes back, and their hearts open to the incredible message.

Stephen's friend, Nicolaus, is actually a Gentile whom Stephen had led into Judaism. He had been circumcised and was a devout believer.

These are the Hellenists, Jews who speak Greek as their primary language. Philip is astonished: even the Greek-speakers with their cosmopolitan lifestyles are eager to believe! It is a world turned upside down. Because of the peculiar nature of Jerusalem in Jesus' day, the Good News must be preached in two different languages right from the start. For there are people present in the Temple audience who have never learned Aramaic.

Jerusalem is a city of two distinct language groups. This fact about the Jerusalem in which the earliest Church begins her journey is worth stressing because it will play a major role in the development of the Church, a role that no one was expecting.

How had Jerusalem become divided like this, and what had happened to Hebrew? Many centuries before, the Babylonians had conquered Palestine, Egypt, Syria, and big parts of Asia Minor, present-day Turkey. Most of the Jews had been driven from the Holy Land into exile. They were taken east as a captive people, and they lived in Mesopotamia for many years. They learned the language of their conquerors, the international language, Aramaic. As the years passed they stopped using Hebrew, except for a few who made a study of it. In their homes and their places of business, the Jews spoke the language of the Babylonians.

When the Persians conquered Babylon, they allowed the Jewish exiles to return home. There in Palestine, the international language, the language both Babylonians and Persians used, became the common language. That continued down to Roman times in Jesus' day. So Jesus himself spoke the lingua franca of the Babylonians and the Persians: Aramaic. So did the Apostles and the disciples. So did Jesus' audiences. Jesus was an event among those who spoke Aramaic.

Hebrew was still used in the Temple worship, and in parts of the synagogue service, but most of the service was in Aramaic. The Hebrew Scriptures were translated into Aramaic so the people could understand them.

But some of the Jews had not gone to the east at the time of the invasions. They had fled to Egypt, and to Syria and to Asia Minor. There they remained throughout the period of Persian dominance. Then came Alexander the Great. He conquered the Persian Empire, and he brought with him all the "glory that was Greece." He introduced the Middle East to Greek art and poetry, the Greek pantheon of gods and goddesses, and Greek architecture. Greek became the language of many parts of the empire. So it came about that the Jews who were resident in Egypt began to speak Greek. The Jews in Asia Minor and even in the coastal cities of Palestine switched also as the generations passed. They knew no Aramaic. A couple of generations after Alexander even the Hebrew Scriptures were translated into Greek.

These were the "Diaspora," Jews scattered throughout the Mediterranean world with their synagogues, living in the midst of the pagans. In some cities they were so many that they had their own quarter, but their businesses brought them into constant contact with the pagans, and they became familiar and at home in the Hellenistic world. They kept their faith in the One God of Israel, and many were very devout. For the great feasts, efforts were made to return to Jerusalem and worship on the Temple-mount.

Little by little, some drifted back to Jerusalem to take up a permanent residence there. Perhaps it was an aging parent whose children were all doing well, and she wanted to spend her last years in the Holy City. Sometimes the children would come and end up staying on. Jerusalem had that power of attracting Jews. It was David's city and Mount Zion, with the Temple and all its splendid ritual.

But there is a problem because the common language in Jerusalem at that time is Aramaic, and many of those returning home from Egypt or Syria know no Aramaic. Nor are they eager to learn it for it is of little use to them. When those who speak no Aramaic come on pilgrimages, they keep together. Each time they visit they stay in the same part of town, and are welcomed by the same hosts who had taken them in on their last visit. So there are various localities inside Jerusalem where there are many who know Greek.

In time, synagogues are built for the Hellenists where Greek is spoken just as it was spoken in their synagogues back in Egypt. Jews had been living in Alexandria for three centuries. It was about as near to Jerusalem as Antioch, and you could make most of the trip by water. Pilgrimages from Alexandria to Jerusalem become so frequent that a special lodging-house was built in Jerusalem, so that Hellenist visitors could feel perfectly at home. There you have facilities for the ritual washings, and a library, and a synagogue, and teachers are provided who explain the Law—all in Greek. Why, then, learn Aramaic?

Anyone from Alexandria who decides to take up a permanent residence in Jerusalem finds an abode near the Alexandrian synagogue. A whole day can go by without hearing a word of Aramaic. Some of the other diaspora groups from Asia Minor and from Greece did the same. So it turned out that the Jerusalem of the Apostles' day is dotted with synagogues and small communities where Greek is spoken. Of course, some of these people do get to know Aramaic just as some of the Jews who were born and raised in Jerusalem learned Greek. But there were many who knew only one of the languages.

When the apostles begin to preach in the Temple their whole focus is on the people of Israel. They are not thinking of a mission to the world. There is no time for that. The end is coming on fast. Israel must be called to repent at once, and to acknowledge the risen Messiah before it is too late.

But right away the problem arises: many Jews cannot hear our message. Some of the Hellenists who hear the Apostles preach are interested in learning more. They want to have it all explained to them in Greek. Philip and Andrew are called upon to take care of them. Philip and Andrew take to preaching in Greek whenever the other apostles preach in the Temple in Aramaic. What joy among the disciples: the message is spreading among the Hellenists. They are a class of people so different from the Galilean disciples.

The fact that they speak Greek is only the most obvious of the differences. Whereas the world of the disciples is Galilee and it is an event for them just to visit Jerusalem, for many of these Greek-speaking Jews, Jerusalem is a quiet, out-of-the-way place, a good spot to avoid the distractions of the great Roman world that they had known. They are pilgrims seeking a more intense pattern of devotional life; their roots are elsewhere.

On returning to Jerusalem, they find the Temple priests singularly unattractive for their way of exploiting the pilgrims. At the same time, the intellectual arrogance of the Pharisees, and their casuistic interpretations of the Torah are not attractive either. In their own synagogues, their focus is on the basics: the universal nature of God's choice of the Jews. They see themselves as bearers of a truth that all people need, even their non-Jewish neighbors. Their years in Alexandria or Philippi have made them conscious of the relationship between their faith and the whole world. Instead of ritual law, they focus on philanthropy and the basic Ten Commandments.

They are a rather devout group. That is why they have returned to Jerusalem. They love being near the Temple, and the Torah plays a major role in their lives. In a way, they resemble the Jews of an earlier age, before the casuistry and the excessive concern for ritual law had set in.

It is no wonder the apostles are delighted when Philip tells them about Stephen and Nicolaus. As the days go by Stephen brings more of his friends to join the disciples. Nicolaus, too, proves to be an eloquent preacher. The message which fills the disciples' hearts is being welcomed among a people so different from them, a group with much greater prestige and know-how, cosmopolitan and devout at the same time. It is a marvel and a source of great assurance that it is indeed the Spirit of God at work in their words.

What attracts this sophisticated audience? Why do they listen to these "backwoodsmen"? Perhaps it is this new emphasis on the spirit over the letter of the Law. This invitation to freedom is what they have been looking for. How welcome to them is the insistence that cleanliness is a matter of what comes out of the heart, not what goes into the mouth. How delightful to find, at last, a focus on the active love of the neighbor over the other commandments—even the Sabbath law. The new law that rises above the scribal way of thought and frees them from being tied down to the letter—that is what they have been seeking for in vain in the Jerusalem of priests and Pharisees. They join the disciples in considerable numbers and the group of believers is greatly encouraged.

But the entry of all these people who cannot understand Aramaic creates problems for the disciples. What to do at the supper services? These Hellenists can't get a thing out of the talk in Aramaic. The lack of a common language guarantees that the new group will never totally mix with the "old"! Sharing is too cumbersome. Those who know both languages become very busy.

How suddenly the Apostles are faced with a major problem! Two groups divided by a language barrier in what is still a community of just a few hundred members. Both groups continue attending the Temple services and their own synagogues. That is no big problem. It's when they come together on their own for supper that the problem develops. Those who speak Greek—the "Hellenists"—have always attended services in synagogues where Greek is spoken. The other group—the "Hebraists," a much larger group that includes the Apostles—have been attending services in Aramaic. But now these peoples of two different worlds are meeting together at table, at a ritual meal, and a major language barrier arises.

The solution that is adopted is the same one used in the synagogues: begin a new supper-gathering for those who can't understand Aramaic. Who will be the leaders? How will they keep in touch with the Apostles? For it is the Apostles and those who had been with Jesus during his public career who have the memories that are now precious to all the believers.

Seven leaders are chosen, all of them, of course, Greek-speakers, and one of them is the Apostle Philip. But the leader of the new assembly is not an Apostle! He is the man filled with zeal and passion, Stephen. He has already proven himself outstanding in preaching to the Hellenist Jews, and conversing with them. His work has produced many converts.

After the seven are chosen, the Apostles come forward and lay hands upon them. One of the seven is Nicolaus, the first Gentile to enter the Church.

Let us take a closer look at the Hellenist gathering and its Greek-speaking members. They are very conscious of the great world of the Gentiles. For them, the Gentiles are not just people you saw rarely and never spoke to. They have been co-citizens of theirs in the great cities of the Empire. They know them as neighbors, competitors in business, and partners in civic enterprise. This has shaped their outlook. They do see themselves as the chosen people of God, but they are aware of being there for the Gentiles also. They have encountered many God-fearers among the Gentiles, and they have welcomed these non-Jews into their synagogues.

Some of them had heard Jesus himself, and been attracted. As they listen in the Temple to these men from Galilee with their country ways and speech, they are impressed. The enthusiasm and the assurance of these preachers is overwhelming. It is infectious. Stephen too is filled with an eloquence and grace that is difficult to resist. They want to learn all they can of Jesus, and of his teaching.

Were we to find a time-warp that would enable us to spend a few days in Jerusalem in the summer and fall of AD 30, what would surprise us most would be how Jewish this earliest Christianity is. They take part in the Temple ritual with no sense that this has lost its meaning. What would it be like to see John praying devoutly near where a large bull is being killed and cut up for burning! They meet in their synagogues and find the services quite comfortable. We would have to look very carefully to find the differences between these Christian communities and any other community in town.

If we joined them for supper, we would notice the difference. At table there is that unique ingredient in the practices of these new groups. It is a strange ritual element. We have mentioned the intense curiosity of the early believers, especially the newly converted, to hear every anecdote about Jesus. His sayings and his activities are recounted, and the memories of those who had witnessed his life are constantly being probed. Every detail of his life and his passion are searched out. The new believers are never satisfied. It's like hearing an old uncle tell you a story about your father as an adolescent. You can't get enough. You even wonder how they could have forgotten anything.

At table, over the meal, the eyewitnesses recall this incident and that one, and then link them up with the essential message, even items that seem unimportant, or a saying that the speaker himself did not understand when he first heard it.

As they speak of Jesus' sufferings, and as they describe the last meal together, they take a piece of bread as Jesus had done, and repeat the words he had used as best they can remember them. Then, a cup of wine. And then the command: "Do this in memory of me." People cry out, "Come, Lord Jesus!"

In the Hellenist gathering, the same takes place. But someone has had to translate it all into Greek. All the anecdotes, the sufferings, the ritual at the supper have been translated into Greek.

This puts a big burden on the bilinguists, Philip and Andrew. Others of the Apostles' followers, like Barnabas and John Mark, who knew Greek, have joined the Hellenist community also.

These bilinguists are to play a vital role in the first few months. They are the beginnings of what is to come. Everything that is known about Jesus must be translated into Greek. Every anecdote is welcomed. The new believers cannot get enough.

Whenever we set to the work of translation, decisions have to be made: we are confronted with options. The words Jesus used at the supper contain a striking instance of this problem.

One of the Aramaic words that Jesus had used—*bisra*—could be translated into Greek in two ways, for the Greek language has two different words, *sarx* and *sōma*. *Sarx* is much like our "flesh," and *sōma* is like the English "body." The translator must decide which one to use. One narrator, a close follower of Jesus, says this: "My flesh for the life of the world." Another narrator says: "This is my body for the life of the world." When you translate, you are forced to choose, and this requires reflection: which is the better word? Because of the entry of the Hellenists, the early Church is forced into translating, and into reflecting about what is being said. Had they remained in Galilee, or had they found that few Greek-speakers joined them, they could have avoided the reflecting. But as it is, they cannot avoid it, and it will make a difference in the way the Church develops.

Given the existence of two language groups, and the need to translate everything, the translators are forced very early on to do some reflecting about the precise meanings of the words they are using. But in the group around the Apostles, the Aramaic-speaking synagogue, this is not a major concern. They simply use the same word that Jesus used, *bisra*. What might be the best word in Greek is not a problem for them. But among the bilinguists there are efforts by different people, reflections about the proper choice, and discussions among the translators. The Hellenists form a very small congregation, but they are into the precise meaning of words much more than the Apostles.

How few weeks have passed since Jesus was put to death. Yet so much is happening. Things are getting out of hand, in a sense. The Apostles cannot be on top of everything, nor do they try. There is a deep eagerness on the part of all believers to listen to the Apostles. They want to pick their brains, to get out of them every possible memory. In that sense, their authority is immense. But decisions are being made by others also, and some of these decisions are going to prove vital.

The movement has left its home in Galilee. In Jerusalem it has been surprised by the entry of people who do not speak their language. Within weeks there are two supper-gatherings, separated by language and cultural differences, but they are one in their sentiments and their faith. The seed is growing rapidly, and changing rapidly in ways no one has expected. In the coming chapters we will explore these very first steps in greater detail.

3

Hearing the Scriptures Afresh

The disciples were expecting a breaking in on human history just as the Qumran community did. But Qumran prepared for it by settling in a remote plateau on the shores of the Dead Sea. Had the disciples of Jesus chosen that path, they could have purchased the hillside where Jesus preached the Beatitudes, and there set up a few small huts as they waited eagerly for the change. They would have done just enough work to keep themselves alive from day to day—fishing, getting water, etc. Most of the day would be spent in prayer and work. Nothing from the outside would have disturbed the steady flow. But that option was rejected.

Nor did the disciples separate themselves from the traditions. But what if they had chosen to ignore Scripture? What if some eloquent disciple had made a most persuasive case for focusing only on Jesus as the entire word of God: "What need have we for all these texts from the Age of the Shadow? We now live in the presence of the Light." One idea alone would have been at the center of the group consciousness, an anticipation of the return of Jesus in triumph. But that option was also rejected.

They did engage in dialogue with those outside the sect. They did sit and listen to the Scriptures as to God's word. The community deliberately entangled itself in a dialogue with the texts they were hearing, and with the people they preached to.

Those two patterns were not an inevitable part of any path they could have taken but they were the choices of the group. These choices provided them with an outside stimulus that forced the community along a path of constant reflection. It will get them into situations from which they cannot extricate themselves except by going forward into unknown territory. The presence of this irresistible need to reflect will squeeze them forward out of their familiar world like a butterfly out of its cocoon.

The disciples go to the Temple each day, and hear the reading of the Scriptures. At every synagogue service that they attend, they hear more of the texts of Scripture. All their lives they have been doing this, but now it is a new experience for them. Many of the texts have been read often before, but while the texts are the same, the disciples who hear them have changed.

Within the first few days of their arrival back in Jerusalem, while he is attending the Temple service in the morning, one of the disciples of Jesus listens as the choirs sing Psalm 118.

> This is the LORD's own gate,
> through it the righteous enter.
> I thank you for you answered me,
> you have been my savior.

He becomes a bit drowsy as the chanting continues but the next verse wakes him up. The choir sings:

> The stone which the builders rejected
> has become the cornerstone.
> By the LORD has this been done;
> it is wonderful in our eyes.

Once, in the midst of a great argument with the Pharisees, Jesus had used that verse. On goes the chanting, but the disciple is now alert.

> This is the day the LORD has made;
> let us rejoice in it and be glad.
> LORD, grant salvation!
> LORD, grant good fortune!

And then the alternate choir:

Blessed is he who comes
in the name of the LORD.
—Psalm 118:20-26

The disciple is now wide awake. What a great text! It will be perfect for the supper-ritual where it will be his turn to recite the words Jesus used at the Last Supper.

Thus Psalm 118 became the first Scriptural text to be added to the few words of the supper-ritual. That evening, just before he takes up the bread, and as everyone quiets down, he sings out the familiar verse: "Blessed is he who comes in the name of the Lord!" And the community repeats it. A stray text has found its way into the Eucharist, and it has remained there ever since.

Imagine Peter's experience as he sits in the Temple and hears them sing this psalm:

For it is not an enemy that reviled me—
that I could bear—
Not a foe who viewed me with contempt—
from that I could hide.
But it was you, my other self,
my comrade and friend,
You, whose company I enjoyed,
at whose side I walked
in the house of God.
—Psalm 55:12-14

Many texts like this one take on new meanings for the Apostles and the close disciples of Jesus. It becomes easy for them to believe that everything had been seen beforehand, and spelled out clearly in advance. As they listen to Scripture it is like hearing someone commenting on the spectacular events of these last few months. It is as if all of Scripture has been written to throw light on what has just occurred.

Very early on, certain texts take on a central significance for Jesus' followers. The first is Psalm 110. Imagine a disciple of Jesus listening to this text, one evening in the synagogue, a few weeks after the terrible Passover.

> The LORD said to my lord:
> 'Sit at my right hand
> while I make your enemies your footstool.'
> —Psalm 110:1

For the disciple its meaning is clear: David is having a vision of a conversation. The LORD, God himself, is speaking to someone whom David calls "my lord." This lofty personage who is worthy of being called "lord" by David himself, is also somehow David's own lord.

Given the events of the last few months, the reference to Jesus is overwhelmingly obvious. Jesus is the Lord! That is the very phrase they are already using. They had called him "lord" while he was alive: *marē*ʾ. Now he is alive again, and they are calling him "lord" again in their spontaneous prayers.

As the disciple listens to Psalm 110, he hears it as a prophetic description of Jesus' being exalted. David had seen Jesus being raised to God's right hand—that's what his rising from the dead means! It will quickly become a favorite text in both assemblies. Even the Greek-speakers will use the Aramaic word for "lord" in some of their prayers. It is what his close followers had called Jesus.

Almost at once one of the disciples sees a connection between Psalm 110 and a text from the Second Book of Samuel, a text that has been very popular among all devout Jews who are expecting the end-time. Nathan, the prophet, is speaking to David the words of God:

> The LORD also declares to you
> that the LORD will make a house for you;
> when your days have been completed
> and you rest with your ancestors,
> I will raise up your offspring after you,
> sprung from your loins,
> and I will establish his kingdom.
> He it is who shall build a house for my name,

and I will establish his royal throne forever.
I will be a father to him,
and he shall be a son to me...
Your house and your kingdom are firm
forever before me;
your throne shall be firmly established forever.
—2 Samuel 7:11-14, 16

Here is the explanation behind David's calling the exalted Jesus his own lord in Psalm 110. Jesus is this heir, sprung from David's loins. It fits nobody else. He has just entered into an everlasting kingship. Jesus is that son of David seen by Nathan in his prophetic vision centuries before. It is obvious to the disciple as he listens. He is eager to show the others how clear it is, how convincing it is once you see it spelled out. How could they themselves have missed it when the texts are so explicit!

The disciples are not completely aware of it, but there is much going on within them, much that is confused, much that seeks for words. As they listen to the texts, they are alert for whatever will help them express their innermost convictions. They are busy like Walt Whitman's spider.

A noiseless patient spider,
I mark'd where on a little promontory it stood isolated,
Mark'd how to explore the vacant vast surrounding,
It launch'd forth filament, filament, filament, out of itself,
Ever unreeling them, ever tirelessly speeding them.[6]

Every so often as they listen, a phrase comes into their consciousness and it echoes with some deeper reality within them.

The disciples were surrounded by a strange world. They searched for familiar things that they could relate to, both for their own understanding, and because their hearers needed it.

Their own hearts are filled to bursting. With delight they uncover echoes in the Scriptures, echoes their ears had not been able to hear until now.

As these echoes multiply, and as they find in the most unexpected places more and more toe-holds for the filaments they have launched, they get the sense that Someone has planted all these connections long before. Or even that Someone had been himself launching forth filaments down through the ages, and finally the filaments had found a people with many toeholds.

There is present in Nathan's prophecy another element that finds a powerful echo in the consciousness of the disciples. It is in these words: "I shall be a father to him, and he shall be a son to me." Jesus had called God by the word *'abba,* "father," a word that has intimacy and affection in it. So he had spoken and prayed, and the disciples cannot forget that way of speaking. Here the prophet is explaining it, many centuries before. God sees in Jesus a son of his own, that very intimate and affective relationship that Jesus felt. Jesus had been conscious of being God's son. God's son! This crucial word must be preached to Israel. As the months pass, nothing else will prove so effective in getting across the good news.

A third note sounded in Nathan's words is the element of kingship. Since Jesus is David's heir, he is a king, too, like his father. But all this is to occur at the end-time when ordinary life will come to an end. This king of the end-time will reign forever, and, in fact, his being king will precisely make it the end-time, his kingship will be such a new thing. Jesus had promised that. He would come soon and the world would be transformed. A delay is allowed only to give Israel time to believe, a pause between the enthronement of Jesus as king which had occurred at his rising from the dead, and his return in all regal splendor. A moment of grace is intervening, and a task is given to his followers: preach the good news to Israel.

Imagine what an experience it is for the early followers, with all of this in the forefront of their concerns, to go to the synagogue service. Imagine them joining in the singing of Psalm 2:

> Why do the nations protest…
> against the LORD and against his anointed one?
> The one enthroned in heaven laughs;
> the Lord derides them,
> Then he speaks to them in his anger,
> in his wrath he terrifies them:
> 'I myself have installed my king
> on Zion, my holy mountain.'
> —Psalm 2:1, 4-6

How obvious is its meaning now! David here is talking of that same event: God has raised up a king. David had called this king "the anointed of the Lord"—the Messiah.

Then David in his vision overhears this Messiah-King speaking of his experience of exaltation by God:

> he said to me, 'You are my son;
> today I have begotten you.'
> —Psalm 2:7

There it is again, explicitly. The Messiah-King is God's own son! To whom had God ever spoken like that? How can a disciple miss it once it is pointed out?

Then David sees in his vision the Messiah-King and Son of God listening as God speaks:

> Ask it of me, and I will give you the nations
> as your inheritance
> and, as your possession, the ends of the earth.
> —Psalm 2:8

His sovereignty is absolute, ultimate, final. He has been appointed king of the end-time.

Who, then, is this Jesus whom they are preaching?

This Jesus whom you all put to death—God has raised him up, and has seated him at his right hand. God has enthroned him as king of the end-time, and all power is now his. God has fulfilled the promises of the prophets. Jesus has been revealed as God's own Son.

How can such spectacular claims be believed? A most unimpressive group of over-intense people with a claim that is simply incredible. And yet it *does* spread. People do join them, let themselves be baptized, and get caught up in spreading it further.

But it is so easily refuted: why would God let the man die? If all of this is so clearly predicted by the prophets, where are these statements to be found? But these early disciples were ready for them.

That this king would be met with unbelief had been predicted!

> Who would believe what we have heard?
> To whom has the arm of the LORD been revealed?
> —Isaiah 53:1

It is hard to believe: the King of the end-time would be rejected! It is mind-boggling. It is amazing that anyone can accept it, but the marvel is taking place. People are being converted.

Imagine how Peter feels as he listens to this reading:

> He grew up like a sapling before him,
> like a shoot from the parched earth.
> He had no majestic bearing to catch our eye,
> no beauty to draw us to him.
> He was spurned and avoided by men,
> a man of suffering, knowing pain,
> like one from whom you turn your face,
> spurned, and we held him in no esteem.
> —Isaiah 53:2-3

The disciples are listening as it is read out in the synagogue. Isaiah even spells out carefully *why* God had allowed Jesus to die.

> Yet it was our pain that he bore,
> our suffering he endured.
> We thought of him as stricken,
> struck down by God, and afflicted,
> But he was pierced for our sins,
> crushed for our iniquity;
> He bore the punishment that makes us whole,
> by his wounds we were healed.
> —Isaiah 53:4-5

That is why he has died, and that is why this text from Isaiah becomes a central text for the disciples right from the beginning. This becomes the quotation they use most often in explaining Jesus' death.

To understand Jesus' strange kingship, you have to be in need of forgiveness. You have to see how far astray you are. Then, his death will fill a great need in your own reality, and the death of the Anointed One will become a blessing. So the early preaching is insistent on the sinfulness of Israel, and its need for forgiveness. It is such an unpleasant truth! Yet the Apostles feel impelled to teach it.

The death of Jesus and his exaltation are seen as already foreshadowed in the Scripture they have been hearing from their youth.

Psalm 16 becomes for one of the disciples a description of the inner experience of Jesus. How else can anyone understand it?

> Therefore my heart is glad, my soul rejoices,
> my body also dwells secure,
> for you will not abandon my soul to Sheol,
> nor let your devout one see the pit.
> —Psalm 16:9-10

Is it possible for an early disciple to hear such a text and not see Jesus and the events of his death and resurrection spelled out there. The texts are useful in helping the disciples see that Jesus' resurrection, an event which had rendered them speechless, actually has a meaning that can be put into words. It can be preached to others because there are images and ideas in Scripture itself that express with a certain precision the significance of Jesus and his death and resurrection.

In some cases, a phrase is discovered, and proves to be of endless use, and lends itself to a rich development. But that is not always the case. Here is an example of a phrase that was soon abandoned. Jesus had used of himself the title, "Son of man." It was a phrase with much obscurity in it. But because he had used it, the disciples use it in the earliest preaching. Soon one of the disciples attaches a section of Psalm 8 to it, to help explain it.

> What is man that you are mindful of him,
> and a son of man that you care for him?
> You made him for a little while
> lower than the angels;
> you crowned him with glory and honor,
> you have put all things under his feet.
> —Psalm 8:6-8

As the disciple hears this psalm, the echoes are everywhere. It begins with God's care for the "son of man," how God is "mindful of him."

Then it describes the abasement of the passion: "You made him for a little while lower than the angels."

Finally his enthronement is spelled out: "You crowned him with glory and honor, and put all things under his feet."

It is similar to the text of Psalm 110, and it is fused with it to make the phrase "son of man" central during these first few weeks.

But the Hellenists soon find the phrase not too useful. It has to be constantly explained, and it is much easier to use titles like "Lord" and "God's own Son" in the preaching. Very soon "son of man" disappears from the preaching, though it is still remembered as the way that Jesus himself spoke. As the disciples tell stories of the life and words of Jesus, his use of "son of man'" is carefully recounted. But it is replaced in the actual preaching of the Good News by more easily understood terms.

The community that is forming has a task: get the word out to the people of Israel—in Aramaic, and in Greek. They are eager to find the best way to put it. They are constantly searching for better ways to explain it, and constantly testing the words being used.

"Son of man" fails the test, but Stephen, the leader of the Greek-speaking synagogue, joins Psalm 110 to another scriptural text in a way that proved to have endless riches in it.

It is a verse of Psalm 110 that is the first ingredient of this new mix.

> Yours is princely power from the day of your birth.
> In holy splendor before the daystar, like dew, I begot you.
> —Psalm 110:3

Now Stephen joins to this a text from Proverbs:

> The Lord begot me, the beginning of his works,
> The forerunner of his deeds of long ago;
> From of old I was formed
> at the first,
> before the earth.
> —Proverbs 8:22-23

At once he senses the tremendous significance.

With this text we are suddenly in a world of superhuman figures. It is quite natural to turn to this type of otherworldly image to explain the impact that Jesus has had on all of them. With his rising from the dead, now they can see that he is not just a part of human history. He is its centerpiece, its ultimate meaning. Everything before leads up to him, and the future will flow from him and toward him. All this they have already sensed. Now they have a text that captures it.

> When there were no deeps I was brought forth,
> when there were no fountains or springs of water;
> Before the mountains were settled into place,
> before the hills, I was brought forth.
> —Proverbs 8:24-25

Unlike the "son of man" of Psalm 8, this text is to prove most useful in helping to grasp the core of the Good News. It is a marvelous discovery: the Book of Proverbs actually shows Jesus talking about himself!

> When the earth and fields were not yet made,
> nor the first clods of the world,
> when he established the heavens, there was I,
> when he marked out the vault
> over the face of the deep;
> then was I beside him as artisan;
> I was his delight day by day,
> playing before him all the while,
> playing over the whole of his earth
> and I found delight in the sons of men.
> —Proverbs 8:26-27, 30-31

It isn't possible for anyone to miss it? This is the same Lord of Psalm 110, the Jesus who has risen. After the glorious confusion that the disciples have been through, here is a text meant for them to hear now. There is delight at finding it, and greater delight in sharing it with others.

Their very devotion to the Temple and the synagogue has exposed these early followers to Scripture. Certain texts explode inside them. It is no longer just the human reader up there, stumbling through. It is God himself speaking. Or the Lord Jesus beginning to speak directly to this group here and now. Jesus has found a way to speak to them most plainly by using texts that they have heard before. Now, they hear them from his lips and they are so precise, so touching, so immediate. As they listen, his presence becomes vivid.

Such are the first steps the disciples take as the weeks pass. They are trying to explain their convictions about Jesus. They use texts their audiences are familiar with. There is a strong sense that they are being led, that Someone had placed markers all along the path for them, that they are following Someone Else's lead. The unexpected riches of Scripture increase their conviction that God is with their mission.

With what energy they hear the Scriptures read! It's like the excitement that happens in a decoding room when someone breaks the enemy code. Everyone is up from the desks, on their feet, eager to be the first to find a new application.

The key to the Scriptures has been given to them in the death and resurrection of Jesus. Wherever they look in the texts that discovery is confirmed.

In our times, a suggestion has been put forward that actually there was no great messianic expectation in Jesus' day. It was the first Christians with their brilliant rereading of Scripture who turned the Hebrew Scriptures into a treasure chest of messianic lore, so that after them no one—whether Jewish or Christian—can read the Old Testament without being influenced by their work.

True or not, it does capture the impact that occurs when the disciples who have witnessed Jesus' death and resurrection come to listen to the texts of Scripture. Almost everywhere they look, Jesus is being spoken of—in the Psalms, the prophets, even in the histories. They become convinced that Scripture had been written precisely to help them understand who Jesus really was.

The filaments they have been launching forth are linking up, and a web of language is being spread to help catch some of the glory they have experienced, and to express it to others.

4

Splitting the Shema

What was the atmosphere in which the earliest disciples lived? The then Cardinal Ratzinger, later Pope Benedict XVI, was quoted years ago as saying that some people think that the Church is a big debating society. Was that true in the case of the earliest Christians? Certainly as the years went by heated discussions did take place, so the tradition to argue does go way back (cf. Acts 15:2).

But the earliest years were quite different. How to capture their experience, and avoid reading back into this primitive scene patterns that developed much later?

You can tell a great deal about the inner life of an organization by the way they debate and the things they consider worth debating about. When the Communists seized power in Russia in 1917, theirs was a rather literate group. Under their belt was a century of theory and debates. Their revered texts were filled with suggestions on how the new world would operate, and how to go about decision-making in the age of the proletariat.

They tried implementing these suggestions as much as they could. At first they even tried having the workers take over the running of the factories. But within a short time, thanks in part to the advance of the hostile reactionary armies, they called back the old management. But that reflexive emphasis on theory remained a constant among Russian Communists as the decades rolled by. Every decision had to be shown as flowing straight from the theory.

But the behavior patterns of the first Christians did not come from theories nor debates nor books. If you wanted to join them, there was no carefully-planned period of indoctrination, there was no catechism to study. It wasn't because the Apostles just didn't have time to write one, but rather the need for one never surfaced. They were in the kind of scene where nobody even thought of it.

You became a Christian within hours—even minutes—of your decision to join. Becoming a Christian involved doing what Christians did. You worshipped with them and joined in their mission to Israel. With that you were as much a full-fledged member as anybody.

The disciples were more like bird-watchers who have seen a rare bird deep in the forest. Once the bird has flown away and the experience is over, they hurry back to tell others of what they saw and where. They want others to have that same experience.

Like Gerard Manley Hopkins, the British and Jesuit poet, on the morning he saw a windhover in windy flight,

> I CAUGHT this morning morning's minion, king-
> dom of daylight's dauphin, dapple-dawn-drawn Falcon, in his riding
> Of the rolling level underneath him steady air, and striding
> High there....[7]

Actually he hadn't *caught* it. He had seen it. He didn't have it in a cage to show it off as his own. It wasn't his. It was its own. So too, the message that came out of the Apostles' encounter with the mystery wasn't theirs. They didn't think of it that way, with such a triumphalist tone. They only knew that they had seen it and where. They had encountered the "Kingdom of daylight's dauphin... in his riding." In their joy they had to tell others. They could not but speak. "We cannot stop proclaiming what we have seen and heard" (Acts 4:20). But theories played no part.

But very early on the disciples were forced to make decisions, and these decisions brought about radical changes. And yet, even when the choices were vital ones, they were often not conscious ones. To the disciples the steps they were taking appeared inevitable. There was no struggle over what was being rejected.

The road they are on suddenly forks, but the direction they must take is so clear that the other option appears a non-option. No one in the car asks, "Which way do we go now?" No one says aloud after the junction has been passed, "Do you think we should have taken the other road back there?" They experience themselves traveling along a straight highway with nothing but dirt roads going off to the side every so often. Often there is no need to pause or to reflect.

There is no clarified process of decision-making because they do not see themselves as making decisions. But decisions are being made, and very early on. One of the vital decisions involves the question of monotheism.

Each day the disciples attend the rituals in the Temple. They are typical devout Jews. Walk into one of their synagogue services, either the one presided over by the Apostles in Aramaic, or the ones where the service is done in Greek, there is little to make you aware of anything radically new. The readings are not original. The usual cycle of Scripture, the usual psalms and blessings, and the form of the service are exactly what you find all over town.

Whatever these people might be up to, they are clearly not interested in separating from the ancient Jewish tradition. There had been sects in Judaism all along, and there is nothing to indicate that this new family is anything more than just another sect, quite at home within the great traditions of Jewish worship.

Even the table ritual at home is somewhat like a Passover meal. It's nothing spectacularly new. Would you have been surprised at the constant remembering of Jesus? He was, after all, the founder of this little sect, and it is quite customary to recall the words and deeds of those who had founded the different sects.

The loud calls of *mar*, the Aramaic for "Lord," may surprise you, especially when this happens in the Greek-speaking synagogue. What may catch your attention as you listen to this oddity more closely is the fact that these calls upon the Lord are not being addressed to God, but to Jesus. And he had died.

"Jesus is Lord." "Come, Lord Jesus." At every service his shocking death is recalled. But there is no lamentation. This awful event, so recent and so devastating, is now mentioned without sorrow. He is being addressed as if still alive. He is being acclaimed as power-filled in this present moment, and as master of the future, a glorious future that is coming soon. Jesus does have a role in the worship of this new sect, and that alone distinguishes it clearly from anything else in Judaism.

An unbending monotheism is the centerpiece of the Jewish faith. It is their great pride that the one and only true God has revealed himself to them, while the pagan empires wallow in superstition and unbelief. Jews are identified by their refusal to take other gods into their Temple. Throughout the Roman Empire special laws are in effect giving Jews a place all their own. They do not have to worship the state gods.

Their peculiar religion is a source of constant friction with the Gentiles. Any suggestion of an assault upon their faith is met with disturbances, especially in Jerusalem itself. Riots had developed when one day some shields were set up in front of Herod's palace. The inscriptions on the shields were dedications to the gods of the Romans! On another occasion imperial standards were raised inside the fortress Antonia. On the standards were medallions with the images of the gods! Another riot broke out when a Roman guard, on the roof of one of the Temple walls, made an obscene gesture. Worshipping the one and only God is a most sensitive point for Jews.

This unyielding commitment to monotheism is summed up in the most sacred profession of faith, the Shema:

> Hear, O Israel! The LORD is our God, the LORD alone! Therefore, you shall love the LORD, your God, with your whole heart, and with your whole being, and with your whole strength. Take to heart these words which I command you today. Keep repeating them to your children. Recite them when you are at home and when you are away, when you lie down and when you get up. Bind them on your arm as a sign and let them be as a pendant on your forehead. Write them on the doorposts of your houses and on your gates (Deuteronomy 6:4-9).

In the same book very strict regulations are set down in the Lord's name. They enjoin the total destruction of any tribes that Israel defeats in war. "Put them under the ban... do not be gracious to them" (Deut. 7:2). "You shall not intermarry with them,... for they would turn your sons from following me to serving other gods" (verse 4). "You shall consume all the peoples which the LORD, your

God, is giving over to you. You are not to look on them with pity, nor serve their gods, for that would be a snare to you" (verse 16).

Even the captured silver and gold was seen as a dangerous temptation to idolatry.

Later when Saul routs the Amalekites, he takes Agag, the king, captive. "But the rest of the people he destroyed by the sword, putting them under the ban" (1 Samuel 15:8). "Then the word of the LORD came to Samuel: 'I regret having made Saul king, for he has turned from me and not kept my command'" (verses 10-11). There is to be no other god but the LORD alone. Agag must be killed.

The disciples of Jesus still recite with simple faith the Shema: the LORD is our God, the LORD alone. But at the supper-ritual the title "Lord" is being used of Jesus, the founder of their sect, a man who had lived so recently, and had died so shamefully. How can that most sacred title be given to a dead carpenter! How can a faithful Jew split the Shema like that!

There had been great human figures in the past, like Moses and Abraham, and they are greatly esteemed, but they play no role in worship. They are never made the object of cultic veneration. If you are a devout Jew, when you come to pray, you face God, the LORD, and him alone.

Here, in these small groups, a human who has lived and died as all other humans, and who has in fact been executed as a criminal, is being treated as only God has been treated. They are calling upon him because they believe that he is still alive. They are calling upon him now to use powers that he never displayed when he was alive! They call upon him to come again into the world, and bring with him a glorious future.

All the blessings that the true believer looks to God alone for, they look to Jesus for. Isn't this the end of true monotheism? How can these people attend the Temple worship? How can they be present at any synagogue service where the Shema is recited?

What are they thinking of? What is going on inside their heads? It is so paradoxical. They are clearly into something two-fold, binitarian, God and Jesus.

But they keep on going to the Temple and the synagogue, and the supper-ritual. They do see themselves as strict monotheists! For them there is only one God. But this one God has spoken and acted, and is even now speaking and acting in Jesus in an unsurpassable, final, ultimate form. They see Jesus as the fulfillment of the promises of the covenant. He is the one, only, absolutely necessary mediator of salvation. He is what the one God was up to right from the beginning. He has now entered into power. He has the future of all within his will.

The one, true God is being redefined. Now God is seen as having a unique relationship to this Jesus, the crucified. God has poured his power and authority into Jesus. He has made Jesus the one everyone must deal with. All the great hopes that God had raised among his chosen people are being realized only in Jesus. In a sense, it is God himself who has moved Jesus into the foreground. To get God's help, you have to go to Jesus.

For this reason, they call on him as Lord, and they feel justified in doing it. It is still monotheism. There is only one God. But this is what that one God wants! They feel they have no choice. It has been made so plain to them. Their worship of the one God is to include a reverence for Jesus that is unparalleled in Judaism.

How has it come about that these devout Jews are modifying their monotheistic cultus so as to include a Lord who is quite clearly human? This can be explained only by looking at the events they have been through, centering on Jesus of Nazareth.

He had announced that salvation was imminent, that God is their most fond, most concerned father. That proclamation, and his living it out, had the effect of making him the centerpiece of God's plan. They had listened to his preaching and been caught up in it, and then they had witnessed his destruction. He had been swept aside before their very eyes. But, had that been all, there would have been no more to the story, there would have been no "earliest Church."

Something had happened after his death and burial. It began with finding that his body was gone from the tomb they had placed it in. It involves unforgettable moments when Jesus appears alive to his followers. It becomes obvious to them that, despite his death, Jesus was God's supreme word, and is now endowed with God's own power. What he had said must be recalled, what he had commanded must be done, and in every need they must turn to him.

They are deeply humbled men. As they recall the events of Jesus' life, they remember how they had been blind to what he was up to, how they had succumbed to the unique temptation to abandon him at the crucial moment when he needed them most. Their guilt is only a few months old, as is their assurance of forgiveness. It is all very fresh. Just as their experience of guilt was intense, so the joy of being forgiven and taken back into Jesus' company has been overwhelming. This deep sense of guilt fills their preaching with a strange authority. They have spectacular news: salvation and forgiveness for all, no matter how great the sin.

Jesus has died and he was raised. His message had been apparently discredited by his shameful death, but now it has been, in a most stunning way, guaranteed. At the table ritual they recall Jesus' death, and how necessary that death was for them to be forgiven. They call upon him, now in full power, and they acclaim his imminent return.

Their pattern of behavior is not the result of profound reflection. It comes out of the experience they are having. They cannot do otherwise.

They have entered a strange world. Had they been left to figure out what to do, they would have been paralyzed. The events of Jesus' death and resurrection are without precedent. How to respond to such events is being given to them step by step; they are being led. They know from moment to moment what to do, and how right it is to do it.

During his life, Jesus had preached with an enthusiasm, an eschatological anticipation that is hard for us to imagine. Its effect had been extraordinary. He proclaimed himself to be the ultimate word of God. This was the basis for his authority, and he was denounced for these pretensions. He had seen a rare bird of incredible beauty. He had been eager to tell of this wondrous secret hidden from the foundation of the world.

In the resurrection events, the disciples have been led to hear Scripture in a new light: God's prophetic word revealing human sin, and promising deliverance. Scripture is yielding up its secrets: the sufferings of Jesus have been contained there all along, as has his exaltation, and the forgiveness he brings.

The risen Jesus has spoken to them with authority. There is no place for any reasoning, but only for accepting the mission given to them: bring to Israel a last opportunity before the end.

Just as the vigorous enthusiasm of Jesus had infected the disciples, now their own enthusiasm sets the mood of the earliest communities. To be present at the synagogue service, and especially at the table ritual, is to be engulfed in an intense atmosphere. It is similar to the intensity that possesses people on a sinking ship, a fullness of experience that is worlds apart from day-to-day living. Among the earliest disciples, there is this joyous anticipation. Something spectacular and decisive is about to happen, and a new life filled with glory is on the doorstep.

The whole congregation is caught up in it. It feeds on the experience of being together. What is going on inside of one person is echoed when another speaks, or prays aloud, or sings, or calls on the name of Jesus.

They feel "sent." They have become messengers, apostles. He is the divinely chosen one, and through him the eschatological hopes are to be realized. Israel must be given a chance to hear it, to accept it or reject it finally.

That same sense of mission that had impelled Jesus to leave Nazareth is now present in his disciples. His spirit is on them. They have taken the first opportunity when all of the Jews are gathered, and they have left Galilee to confront Israel.

They invade the Temple and they preach to the crowds of worshippers. People come forward to join their group. As an initiation, they use the baptismal rite that John had employed. It signifies the entry into the redeemed community, and the forgiveness of sins.

But there is something very different about this baptism. Each of the newly converted is baptized into the name of Jesus. None of the sects of Judaism had put anyone but God at the center of the initiation process. But here is a cultic setting, and Jesus is given the prominent place.

In the same baptismal ceremony, the convert signifies his or her faith by calling upon the name of Jesus as the believers do at their gatherings. The members of these earliest communities are becoming identified as "those who call upon the name of Jesus" in their assemblies.

The disciples are Jews, devout Jews. They are monotheists, strict monotheists. What if someone asks them: what of your cultic practices where Jesus of Nazareth is your central focus, how is that compatible with Temple worship? But no one asks. They did not yet have words for answers to questions that hadn't yet been asked.

They knew there was only one God, and that unshakeable conviction filled their Temple prayer with meaning. They knew what Jesus had commanded them to do at the supper table, and that command filled the supper-ritual with meaning. Without much thought about theory, they were experiencing God in these two ways from day to day.

Everyone in the Temple was, like them, a believer in the One God. Everyone at the supper was, like them, a disciple of Jesus.

5

A Difference

They call their founder "Lord." That difference in the midst of so many similarities is the tip of the iceberg. Underneath that variation is hidden—even to the eyes of the disciples—the radical newness that their faith contains.

The presence of the disciples in the Temple and the synagogues is not a pose assumed for purposes of infiltration. They still think of themselves as part of the Jewish religion, as its fulfillment. Each day when the services in the Temple end, they do preach, as did the members of the various sects within Judaism. This astonishes no one. At the suppers the difference emerges, but only disciples are present. None of them notices the slight half-step that has been taken.

Everyone present is in the midst of the same overwhelming event. They are like those few people in New York City who go out on the streets the morning after a massive snowfall. Everyone is friendly. They are sharing a moment to remember, and they delight in making remarks about it.

It was like this, too, at a high school football game I saw recently. The home team was behind 7-28 going into the final period. They had made every mistake. Suddenly it changed and they started clicking. 14-28. With six minutes to go they scored again, 21-28. The fans were ecstatic. An event was in the making. They were glad they had stayed on. With twenty seconds left in the game, the home team was first and goal on the visitors' four-yard line. Even though they lost, once the clock ran out people began to babble, wandering about talking to perfect strangers, breaking into any conversations they could. Ordinary inhibitions slipped away.

Such is the atmosphere of these early Eucharistic meals. They are meals shared by people who have been present at a spectacular event, and who are awaiting an even more spectacular one. The urge to share their experience is strong. While the Temple worship is a structured affair and the synagogue services are thoroughly scripted, the suppers are quite informal. That leaves plenty of room for the disciples to share their faith.

As they recall the words of Jesus, the emotion rises. Some of them had heard these Eucharistic words spoken by Jesus himself only a few months before. Their sense of his presence is strong. At any moment, the curtain separating him from them is about to be drawn back.

In the Book of Joel there is a rather precise description of what to expect and what to do when the end comes. This passage may have been the reading in the Temple that morning. Imagine how a disciple of Jesus would feel as the reader read out.

> It shall come to pass
> I shall pour out my spirit upon all flesh.
> Your sons and daughters will prophesy,
> your old men will dream dreams,
> your young men will see visions.
> Even upon your male and female servants,
> in those days, I will pour out my spirit.
> —Joel 3:1-2

That part of the prophecy is already being fulfilled.

> I will set signs in the heavens and on the earth,
> Blood, fire, and columns of smoke;
> The sun will darken,
> the moon turn blood-red,
> before the day of the LORD arrives,
> that great and terrible day.
> Then everyone who calls upon the name of the LORD will escape harm.
> For on Mount Zion there will be a remnant
> as the LORD has said,
> and in Jerusalem survivors whom the Lord will summon.
> —Joel 3:4-5

It is spelled out for all to know. The Spirit is being poured out and visions and dreams and prophesyings are the result. On that great and final day those who call on the name of the Lord will be saved, the faithful remnant in Jerusalem.

So now at the supper one of the disciples arises and recites the Joel text from memory, and some in the group act upon the suggestion in the text and call upon the name of the Lord, their Lord, Jesus. "Jesus is Lord!" For a disciple to declare with his mouth that Jesus is Lord, is experienced by the congregation as an unequivocal sign of the Spirit at work within the heart.

Sensing the nearness of his coming, people cry out spontaneously, "Come, Lord Jesus!" "*Marana tha*!" In a very short time, it becomes usual for the celebrant to start with the invitation, "Come!" and the congregation responds, "Come!"

On occasion, the enthusiasm in the heart expresses itself in "tongues," a rhythmic, melodic outpouring of sounds with no clear meaning, an outburst and overflow of joy.

One evening during the supper among the Greek-speakers, while Stephen is presiding, there is an outburst of speaking in tongues that involves three or four people. In the midst of it, Stephen looks up at the ceiling and his face is transformed. He cries out, "Look! I can see heaven thrown open and Jesus standing at the right hand of God!" To the melodious "tongues" are added cries from around the room, "Come, Lord Jesus! *Marana tha*!" Other visionary experiences occur as the days pass.

What should be made of them? The Apostles are present at some and do not interfere, nor do they caution. This type of experience brings the fervor of the assembly to a peak.

Such experiences confirm the early believers in their conviction that Jesus is now so completely a partaker in God's power and glory that he can appropriately be given a veneration that has previously been reserved for God himself. The visionary and those who are present at the vision and those who hear about it, are profoundly touched, just as in modern times at Lourdes, Fatima, or Medjugorje. It becomes impossible for them to treat Jesus as a past event. "He is risen: he is exalted to God's right hand." He is seen as clothed in glory. All power is his. An alive Jesus, alive and glorified, is accompanying the synagogues and strengthening them.

The enthusiasm that is generated by belief in the gospel message expresses itself well in ecstatic phenomena. The spiritual explosion that marks the earliest Church is an intense joy. One who is haunted by guilt is overcome with an assurance of being forgiven. Add to it the experience of being part of a new family formed in the expectation of an imminent return of the Lord himself, and it is not surprising that the fellowship is flooded with enthusiasm.

The return of Jesus dominates their devotional life. How can it be otherwise? The Easter appearances have placed his return in glory in the foreground of their consciousness.

Faith in a rapidly approaching blessing transforms our experience of the present, and brings with it a joy of anticipation that can equal and even surpass the joy of actually possessing the blessing. The glories of Christmas approaching often surpass Christmas day itself. Winning a lottery can be far more joyful than spending the money. That anticipation-joy is the atmosphere of the earliest communities.

It is an outcome, ultimately, of the joy that Jesus himself had lived. His assurance of the approach of the kingdom and his enthusiastic confidence in God's love for him fired his preaching and stirred his audiences. That trust in his Father that freed and energized Jesus is now being felt by the disciples. The same spirit that flooded Jesus' consciousness is now pouring into their hearts. Each has been invited to call God by that affectionate term, *'abba,* for each one is the object of the Father's concern. In raising Jesus from the dead, God has confirmed the invitation Jesus had extended to all.

They are each and all being invited to imagine themselves seated in glory with the risen Lord, and to know that this image will become a reality soon. It is no wonder that they cannot express themselves in the old patterns. No wonder they find new ways to celebrate. The very disorder and confusion of their gatherings is expressive of a joy that has not yet found words.

Here, then, the sect of the disciples of Jesus does differ from any other sect of Judaism. Jesus is spoken to and called upon just as if he were still alive. A disciple speaks in Jesus' name. Visions of Jesus seated at God's right hand echo the great resurrection appearances. The same words they had heard just a few months before on the lips of Jesus are now heard again. The bread is broken and shared, the cup is passed from hand to hand.

But these supper experiences do not make them lose interest in the Temple. That is the odd fact. They still experience themselves as devout Jews.

Had a Jew who was not a disciple been present, what would he have felt? The differences are so subtle, it may have seemed nothing more than a sect like the Essenes, with a strong devotion to their founder, but still thoroughly Jewish. Seeing the disciples later in the Temple would not have shocked him.

It would have taken a seer or a fortune-teller to see that there was already present a radically new path that would prove incompatible with Temple and with synagogue.

6

Prophesying

The supper-rituals provided the community with an opportunity to develop patterns of experiencing their faith in a group. Besides the acclamations and the speaking in tongues there was another pattern that was called prophesying.

One evening at the supper in the midst of the group experience of Jesus' presence, the Apostle John arises. His eyes are closed in deep concentration. "Listen to what he says who sits at God's right hand." Then he begins speaking in the person of Jesus. "I know your hardships and your poverty. Do not be afraid of the sufferings that are coming to you. Even if you have to die, keep faithful, and I will give you the crown of life for your prize."

What an impact on the disciples! John was so close to Jesus, and now he is saying exactly what Jesus is wanting to say to them. John concludes, "Do not forget my command to you: Love one another."

There are present, of course, those who find it easy to speak. They find the opportunity irresistible. Their love of hearing their own voices at times threatens to dominate the gathering. Perhaps there is an Apostle who never feels satisfied with the spontaneous exclamations of others until he has put it just so, in proper and much needed perspective. His rich strong bass holds the floor drowning out any interrupters.

When he finally perorates, Joanna arises, the wife of Herod's steward. She is one of the women who travelled with Jesus during his days of preaching. In a quiet voice, she begins, "The holy One, the true, who wields David's key, who opens and no one can close, who closes and no one can open, has this to say: I know your deeds and I know your heart. I know the words on your lips. Be on your guard against the yeast of the Pharisees, which is hypocrisy. Among the pagans, their great men lord it over them. They make their power felt. It must not be so among you." How often she had heard Jesus say it; many of the disciples remember it, too.

Some are gifted at this. It begins spontaneously, yet it develops a pattern of its own, like the rap-artists of our day. Sometimes the speaker comes through as false and self-serving and is not approved by the congregation. But some speak, as Jesus had, to the weakness within each, true prophets piercing to the heart. The Apostles lead the way with their deep consciousness of having failed, and their awareness of the danger of self-confidence. "We have all gone astray, each in our own way."

There were no reporters following Jesus around, nor was there an historian commissioned to compile material for a biography. There were just the disciples, and it is their memories that produced our picture of what it was like to be with Jesus during the public life.

As new people joined the community, they were eager to hear from those who had known Jesus well what it had been like to be with him. There were many ears eager to listen to the recollections of the disciples.

Like the close friends of John Kennedy, the Apostles were in demand. After Kennedy's death people were eager to hear the details of his private life. They enjoyed reading about incidents that would give an insight into the "real" Jack Kennedy. This occurs after the death of the famous: those who were nearest to the hero enjoy the spotlight for some time.

Early on it becomes customary to have an Apostle share one of his memories of Jesus with the newcomers who had never been near Jesus. These disciples are envied: they had been able to see his face and hear the emotions in his voice.

Tonight Thomas speaks.

> I remember the afternoon: we were all across the Jordan, there where John had first preached. The authorities were constantly after Jesus. A man came and told Jesus of the sickness of his close friend, Lazarus. And Jesus said, 'Let us go back to Judea.' Someone said, 'That would be suicide.'

> People began trying to change Jesus' mind. 'You'll be killed, Lord!' But he persisted: 'Let us go to him.' So I got this inspiration, and I blurted out: 'Let's go and die with him.' Everyone just stared at me. I realized how naive I was. Then when the chance to die with him came, I slipped back to the Upper Room. Awful!

Often they recall the Last Supper. One night when there are some new converts present for the first time, John recalls the supper. He remembers how Jesus kept insisting he was going to leave them. "When it finally sank in that the Lord was going to leave us, we got into a fight about who would be the new leader." In the silence that follows, the shocked whisper of one of the new people is heard, "You didn't!"

On another occasion Peter tells of a most vivid moment.

> I remember the day when Jesus first began to talk of his death. I pulled him aside. 'You're depressing everyone.' What a fool I was! More than a fool, a tool of Satan. He turned to me in anger: 'Get away from me, you Satan! Peter, you're confusing man's will with God's!'

We know in our own times that sometimes, when the great hero's friends tell incidents from his life, the incidents recounted are not very flattering to the hero himself; but very often are highly flattering to themselves: how they were there, alone with the President, when they worked out the solution to this grave crisis or that one.

But in the case of the Apostles and those who had lived with Jesus we have a very odd outcome. The stories the Apostles told reveal their own shortcomings. Their inability to grasp what Jesus was about is portrayed in marvelous detail.

If we were to read in the memoirs of an aide to Richard Nixon about how he had urged Nixon to keep the tapes when the president was set on destroying them, it might sound credible. The fact that such an admission is embarrassing to the writer makes it somewhat unlikely that he made it up. Among Scripture scholars this is called the criterion of embarrassment. The Apostles related many such embarrassing incidents at those supper-rituals as they recalled what it was like to be with Jesus.

One phrase that was embedded in their memories was "little faiths." Jesus had used it of them often. When they woke him in the boat during the storm, he called them "Men of little faith." Even when Peter walked on the water, Jesus reproached him: "O you of little faith."

One night a disciple told of the day in the boat when Jesus said out loud, "Beware of the yeast of the Pharisees!" The disciples had misinterpreted it to be a criticism of them for not having remembered to bring bread.

When Jesus realized that they had missed the point, he was exasperated. His words burned in their memory. "Why are you talking about having no bread?! Do you still not understand! Are your hearts hardened?"

Why would a disciple tell such a story? Surely they didn't make it up, and it may have occurred on many occasions. "Do you have eyes and fail to see? Do you have ears and fail to hear? You have such little faith!"

Jesus had used that word "still" often enough. "Are even you still without understanding? Do you not realize that everything that enters the mouth passes into the stomach and is expelled into the latrine? But the things that come out of the mouth come from the heart, and *they* defile" (Matthew 15:16). "You still do not know me!" (John 14:9).

This is what it was like to be with Jesus. What it must have been like to hear an Apostle, one of the acknowledged leaders, tell about it at the supper.

One evening Bartholomew tells of a day when he had failed to cure a possessed boy. When Jesus came on the scene, the boy's father told him of his son's problem, and how the disciples had been unable to cure the boy. Jesus was enraged. "How much longer must I be with you?! How much longer must I put up with you?!" He is angry not at the man who had brought the boy, but at the disciples who had not the faith to work the cure.

This was a very rare group of men. In their desire to share their experience of Jesus with others, they were willing to recount the tale of their own unresponsiveness to Jesus' teaching. The enormous energy he had put into getting them to see how shallow their faith was had been an apparent waste. Even at that Last Supper they were still insisting that they did believe. A huge slice of the Gospels is taken up with this one man trying to persuade twelve others that they do not believe him.

Before they come to share the story with the early converts, the Apostles had undergone an eye-opening experience, their behavior during the passion of Jesus. After that confrontation with their own shallowness, the truth that Jesus had urged them to face, without success, now took center stage in each individual consciousness.

At the same time they saw with great precision what Jesus had been trying to do with them, the path of spiritual direction Jesus had been leading them along. They saw it as the only path that would lead to entering the kingdom. They saw that this must be preached to everyone. Out of this staggering realization came the unusual humility of their sharings. In the wake of their cowardice so many pertinent memories were pulled up to the surface, and they could see how hard Jesus had tried to open their eyes to the danger that was coming. He wanted to destroy their illusory self-image. Only if he could get them to see their shallow faith would they be ready to ask for real faith.

On one occasion they do ask for faith. One of the commentators suggests that "The fundamental attitude of a Christian disciple should be 'Grant us more faith.'"[8] Not that there is a pattern of constantly asking for faith on the part of the disciples, but it is clear from their accounts that such asking was what Jesus was hoping to bring about.

Their Calvary experience produced a retrospective clarity about what had been going on. It enabled them to reorder all that had happened, and to focus on those moments that revealed the heart of Jesus' teaching of them. In the experience of being forgiven, "the Spirit brought back to memory all that Jesus had taught them" (cf. John 14:26).

The Apostles were now much like members of Alcoholics Anonymous who have been through the dynamic. When they came to choose a replacement for Judas, they insisted that he be someone who had been with Jesus from the beginning, someone who had taken the entire "training program," someone who knew all the dodges because he had used them himself.

Jesus had not passed out any notes, nor written a book. But now they knew what he had been up to, and the confusion of those years with Jesus took on a unity in their recollections. There was one lesson that had to be learned constantly: honesty, humility.

Their accounts at the suppers were a form of prophesying, revealing what was repellent within the human heart. It was the way to confess the Lordship of Jesus, and in the same story confess the sinfulness that they surrounded him with during his days on earth.

Paul pictures for us the experience of a newcomer at one of these early supper-rituals. People begin to speak in tongues, and the newcomer is shocked and feels they are insane.

But when someone begins to prophesy, like the Apostles, the newcomer finds that he himself is being analyzed, and judged by the speaker. He finds his secret thoughts are being laid bare. He falls on his face and worships God: "God is among you indeed!" In this way the community is testing itself and judging itself, and probing the secrets of the heart, and in this way they renew the experience of forgiveness which is the cornerstone of the good news (1 Corinthians 14:24-25). It would have been so easy for these early followers to have seen themselves as perfect, and in no need of the message of repentance which they preach to others. But this doesn't happen. Their preaching resonates with a self-knowledge that enables them to hear the gospel afresh within their own hearts. These prophetic moments keep them in the real world.

And they do include the call to repentance and the promise of forgiveness in their preaching to the crowds. They take for granted that everyone who hears them needs to hear that message even if, like the Apostles, they will feel strong resistance to it. Jesus is preached as the one who delivers Israel from the bondage of sin.

There is very little in the way of reminiscences in their preaching. That is saved for the suppers. The Temple audience hears of Jesus, the Risen Lord, the Exalted One. The hearers are linked to their ancestors who were also stubbornly resistant to God's will as declared to them by the prophets. Killing the Messiah revealed that same hardness of heart present throughout the history of God's dealings with the chosen people. What amazed the disciples was the eagerness of the crowds and the flow of converts, despite the harshness of the message.

"You stiff-necked people, uncircumcised in heart and ears, you always oppose the holy Spirit; you are just like your ancestors" (Acts 7:51).

As they heard afresh the Scriptures recount the waywardness of Israel, the Apostles were consoled by the persistent refusal of God to turn his back on his flock. How tempted God had been to destroy the people and start over again, but he had refused. He had found a way past their stubbornness. Jesus, too, had succeeded with the Apostles despite their blindness. It meant that the faith they had was grounded in a deep humility, a vivid awareness of their ability to resist.

To the crowds they preached the Good News about a God who like a good shepherd had no intention of letting his stray sheep fall to the wolves. The face of God could only be seen in that context of waywardness. Jesus was welcomed only by the sick.

How did this affect the nature of authority in the community of the disciples? Since Qumran was a much more isolated experience, its authority was much more stable, more institutionalized. In most cult-type settings, the authority of the charismatic founder is passed on to those nearest him. Not quite so gifted with charism as the founder, they preserve their leadership by producing a structure that will protect their dominant position.

At Qumran the authority was quite effectively structured. People knew how disagreements were to be settled, how decisions were to be made. In their chosen isolation the decisions were fewer. Even the dialogue with Scripture did not produce sharp controversy.

But the early disciples of Jesus have a very different experience with leadership. There is a clear authority in those who had known Jesus, but it is compromised by their own histories. Instead of being those who had stood shoulder to shoulder with their founder in his struggle, they are branded, in the very telling of the narrative of Jesus, as men who had misunderstood the heart of his message and eventually failed him when he most needed them.

Their very mediocrity is essential to the revelation of Jesus' reality. Jesus cannot be preached without picturing themselves as failures. That Jesus had been frustrated at their lack of faith in him and had praised the pagans for a faith he had never found among the Apostles is constantly being remembered. A prostitute had grasped the truth long before any of the Apostles did.

This means that their leadership is quite different. Ordinarily the men who stood by the leader are those who receive his mantle. They are the ones who shared his courage and his glory. It is not so with the earliest Church.

These are men no longer confident in their own judgment. That makes for a very different atmosphere in the community. They are the leaders; there's no struggle over that. But they are a humbled crew. The events of the Passover have finally brought them into the truth that they had been blind to. They are very aware of the ease with which they can miss the point. They are open to suggestions—new ways of thinking about the meaning of Jesus, and new words to use in speaking about it. They are quite certain that they do not have the answers to all the questions that come up. They are ready to reach out, to listen to any suggestion.

Neither can any new "sinless" leader emerge, because the Apostles clearly have the authority centered on them. It's a unique situation. Those in whom authority clearly rests are rather discredited, and the very grounds of their humbling is being kept in the forefront of every disciple's consciousness.

They preach the unpleasant truth of the universal need to be forgiven, and that anyone should preach such an unpleasant truth is amazing enough, but even more amazing is that their hearers accept it.

7

The Oddest of the Oddities

The "what-if's" of history. What if Oswald had been hit by a car and killed the night before Kennedy arrived in Dallas? Clark Clifford speculated about that in his autobiography. Would we have avoided the Vietnam tragedy? What if the Southern states had been allowed to leave the Union peacefully? Some years back someone wrote a book on that. What if Napoleon had won at Waterloo? Would it have made any difference at all?

What if just as the Apostles and Jesus began what was to be their last meal together, there was a loud knock on the street door and suddenly up the staircase came the Temple police, and Jesus was arrested right there?

Would it have made any real difference to the development of the earliest Church? Hadn't he already said all that needed to be said? Matthew's Gospel would have lost only a dozen or so verses!

But at that last supper, at the very last possible moment, Jesus did something that was to have a massive impact on the early Christian community. And it actually took only a few seconds. During his public years Jesus had not given any indication that he had an intense interest in inventing a ritual. As the last of the great prophets he had stressed the dangers of hypocrisy in the ritual observances, the tendency to substitute correct rites in the place of love and compassion.

Suddenly at the supper Jesus adds a few original words to the traditional prayer. It appears so casual, but it is a new creation. And he orders the Apostles, "Do this!"

Instead of carefully preparing his apostles for the event, he sprang it upon them. In the Passover-meal setting where he produced his new creation, it took up two very brief moments.

It could easily have been forgotten. The Passover was over for that year; it would not be celebrated for another year. His brief variation on it could have been seen as of minor importance. After all, his washing of their feet had been a striking action, and it had delivered a wonderful message in a rather effective way. And Jesus had commanded his disciples to do the same. But they did not take that command literally. This could have happened with his command to repeat the Eucharist. But it didn't happen.

The Eucharistic command surfaced right away. Peter interrupted an ordinary meal with the suggestion, "Let us do what the Lord told us to do in his memory." The group agreed. Two brief moments of ritual interrupted their table-talk, one early in the supper and the other near the end.

But now these two moments are no longer a part of the Passover ritual. They have lost their setting. Now they occur in the course of a common meal, and it seems quite clumsy. The change of mood from an ordinary meal to such a solemn artificial gesture is abrupt.

Within a few weeks people voice their feeling about the need for a chance to recollect themselves. Some words must be said to set the new mood. Soon Peter adds words that invite people to pause: "Let us remember in silence that extraordinary night. Let us reflect on what we are about to do."

It's not that the table-talk is unseemly, or the least bit worldly. A friend of mine, a liturgical scholar, received permission to perform a type of primitive Eucharist once each semester for his class. All the students were a bit reserved when the meal began. The consecration of the bread took place not long after they had begun. The cup of wine was saved for near the end of the meal. It amazed him to see the effect that framework had on the conversation in between.

It is the same in these earliest liturgies. Of course, at times, anything can occur, even a dispute—as had happened at the supper that night when Jesus was sitting there with them (Luke 22:24).

But even with the mood of peace in which they usually ate, there is still felt a need for some preparing words, and for a bit of time to focus on the reality that is about to become present.

It's not many days before someone suggests the singing of a psalm. "The Lord is my shepherd" is sung. It has such an appropriate reference: "He sets a table before me… my cup overflows." It's providential.

Soon many of the psalms that are used in the Apostles' Temple teaching are sung at the supper-ritual, Psalms 2, 8, 16, and 110. And of course Psalm 118: "Blessed is he who comes in the name of the Lord." Some come forward at each supper to lead in the singing.

But very soon a certain dissatisfaction sets in. Just take Psalm 110.

He crushes kings on the day of his wrath.
He judges nations, heaps up corpses,
crushes heads across the wide earth.

It's not quite the mood of that last meal with Jesus. And what does the next verse mean?

He drinks from the brook by the wayside,
And thus holds high his head.

Each of the psalms has similar problems. The psalms of praise are quite meaningful but they have no reference in them to the heart of the Good News.

The psalms invite the faithful to recall the covenant God made with Israel. At the heart of the covenant are the promises God made to Abraham.

One night God had taken Abraham outside. "Look up at the sky and count the stars if you can. Just so will your descendants be" (Genesis 15:5). That promise had been fulfilled only by crushing kings and "heaping up corpses."

The psalms are filled with reminders. "He struck down many nations, and slew many kings.... He made their land a heritage... a heritage for Israel his people" (Psalm 135:10, 12). That was God's great promise to Israel, the oath "he ratified in a statue for Jacob, an everlasting covenant with Israel: 'To you I give the land of Canaan, your own allotted inheritance'" (Psalm 105:10-11).

Faith in that great promise led to prosperity. "Wait eagerly for the LORD, and keep his way; he will raise you up to inherit the earth" (Psalm 37:34).

Land, children, and a long life. "Who is the one who fears the LORD?... He will abide in prosperity and his descendants will inherit the land" (Psalm 25:12, 13).

But these central promises are ignored by the early disciples. Jesus had distanced himself from them. To try using the psalms to celebrate the Good News was a frustrating job. A verse here or there is strikingly apt, but the rest of the psalm is irrelevant.

The disciples soon feel a certain lack. The psalms are not doing the job. They're not saying what needs to be said.

What is most important is not being spelled out. What the suppers celebrate is the new promise of the gift of the Spirit and eternal life. The covenant with Israel and the great promises on which it had been based are not mentioned at the suppers.

A new promise takes their place, a promise that Abraham never heard, nor Moses. This new promise of life after death was flatly denied in some of the psalms. "The dead do not praise the LORD, not all those who go down into silence" (Psalm 115:17).

Belief in a future life played little or no part in the covenant with Israel. But it is the very centerpiece of the Good News Jesus proclaimed. It is the Apostle John who first offers to write a completely new song.

None of the texts they find in Scripture highlights what is most important. The nail is not being hit on the head. It's like a movie screen when everything is blurred. Something has to be done. Shouts of "Focus!" are heard throughout the theatre.

The psalms and the traditional songs are seen to be inadequate. The ideal song for the supper has to break new ground and use new phrases to describe a radically new vision of life.

It is John who voices the suggestion, "We need a new song that will say precisely what we are about." Many welcome the suggestion at once, but the more conservative hesitate. In the practice of the day, new songs are not a common thing. The liturgies in the synagogue and in the Temple kept to traditional songs.

It's much like the liturgical renewal we have undergone over the last decades. Many were delighted right from the start. But for others the new songs sounded so out of place at the Mass. "It turns me off. I find them distracting."

So too here, James and the more tradition-minded gently raise questions. "It could cheapen the moment." "The songs we are used to work for me."

It's the women who carry the day. "Let's try it out and if it proves a problem, we can drop it." One of the women offers to help John compose the new song. John provides the simple words that express the faith of the community.

Here is that first hymn:

The Messiah is Jesus who died,
Yes! And more—
who was raised from the dead!
He is at God's right hand;
He is interceding for us.

Years later it is quoted by Paul in his Letter to the Romans (8:34). It is such a primitive statement. John stays as close to Sacred Scripture as he possibly can. Two very small steps are taken.

The first small step is the mention of the facts of the "new thing," the Jesus-Event: he died and was raised from the dead. This is the new context of human history. But it is not in the Scriptures. It must be mentioned from now on, for it is the event toward which everything in the Scriptures was aiming.

The second small step is the use of a traditional text and applying it to these two facts: he is at the right hand of God. It's nothing more than a variation of Psalm 110, but now it is given a new setting. It is so placed that it becomes a comment on the Jesus-Event. It now is being used to explain the two facts that are new. The Jesus-Event is narrated first, and then Psalm 110 is used to explain its meaning.

'Sit at my right hand.'
—Psalm 110:1

Then John adds a second text from Scripture. It is a paraphrase of the fourth verse of Psalm 110: "You are a priest forever." It becomes: "He is interceding for us." Jesus is seen as the center of their worship.

How close this song is to the tradition! The only new words are the two primal facts, the Jesus-Event. The rest are words of Scripture, but they have been placed in such a context that they interpret the two facts, and supply them with a very clear meaning.

We are watching the earliest Christian theologian at work, taking the first baby steps. The ropes are being loosened, and the huge liner is gently parting from the dock for a voyage of many centuries of development.

The song is now ready. It will be sung before the sacred words are to be recalled. Simple in its words and in its melody it will be learned easily.

The two composers are, of course, a bit anxious. Early in the meal, when the moment for the blessing of the bread arrives, Peter calls for attention. John gives a brief chant class, and the new song is quickly learned. He leads them through it twice without a hitch. Then they sing it, and Peter recites the words of Jesus. After the bread has been eaten, John intones it again, and all sing it. Afterward the table talk is very assuring. The song is a clear success. Even James is mollified by the careful use of the two Scripture texts. "Besides, it's a rather small concession anyway."

Toward the end of the meal, before the last cup, Peter asks John to lead them again. The easy melody and the simple phrases ring out, for the whole group feels more sure of itself.

Over the next few weeks John and Mary go to work on a second hymn. This one also proves to be a success. Many years later it will be quoted in the Letter to the Ephesians:

> God raised him from the dead
> and made him sit at his right hand;
> and God put all things under his feet
> and made him the head of all things.
> —Ephesians 1:20-22

Once again the first part is nothing but the narration of the Jesus-Event. The "new thing" is expressed—the death of Jesus and his resurrection. Then Psalm 110 is woven in, being seated at God's right hand.

How imprecise is the meaning of the phrase "sitting at God's right hand." It can sound like a retirement to a heavenly stage for Jesus and a disappearance from the human world. But that's not what they meant by it, and John adds a second text from Scripture to spell it out clearly.

Where does he get those last lines from? "God put all things under his feet and God made him head of all things"? Psalm 8, verse 6 is being echoed:

> You have given him rule over the works of your hands,
> put all things under his feet.

How simple and direct! What an easy step to take! Yet it contains expressions filled with possibilities. John has selected his words in such a way that no lid is placed on the Jesus-Event. It is left open to endless development, and that is what he felt inspired to do. He is aware that what is felt and believed cannot be fully expressed. Jesus now hems them in from all sides in a way that has never been known before. There are no words yet to spell out the new experience.

Others of the disciples start to get into the act. There are a number of them who have the necessary skills. But the next song that catches on is a text that Peter makes up, and Mary comes up with an easily learned melody for it.

For some days now Peter has been preaching in the Temple. After each sermon, strangers come up to him to ask questions. As the days pass Peter can't help but notice that one note in his preaching is getting a very rich response, and that note hasn't found its way into either of John's songs. It is a word that arises from deep within Peter's heart. He puts into his song this phrase that he has been using as a refrain: "Jesus suffered once for all."

It isn't in John's hymns. John had stood by the cross with Mary Magdalene, but Peter had been hiding away. Jesus had suffered *for* him. The strangers who are moved by his words keep bringing up that phrase. It touches them too. Here is the hymn Peter writes. Years later it is quoted in the First Letter of Peter:

> Jesus suffered once for all.
> He brought us to God.
> He was put to death in the flesh,
> but made alive through the spirit.

He has gone into heaven.
He is at God's right hand,
with angels, authorities, and powers subject to him.
— 1 Peter 3:18-22

Again we have the basic elements. Peter narrates the Jesus-Event, his death and his resurrection. He adds the good news, the free forgiveness of sins: "Jesus suffered once for all." Then he uses Psalm 110 to describe Jesus' enthronement at God's right hand. He brings in Psalm 8, as had John in his hymn, to assert that all are now subject to Jesus.

With the composing of the first hymns, the Church begins to put some form to what was an experience so profound that speechless awe was its initial effect.

In the first hymns we find an effort to do more than just state the facts of his dying and rising. The composers try to spell out the meaning of the mystery. They have indeed seen someone who was dead and is now walking and talking. But what is that supposed to mean?

What if you visited a cousin of yours in Bethany the week her dear friend Lazarus had died? You were there when they rolled the stone to close the tomb. Three weeks later you come back to town for a visit, and you see Lazarus sitting on his porch chatting with Martha. What a shock!

But what does it mean? It must mean he had an identical twin, or a look-alike relative. Would it enter your head to wonder whether he was the Messiah or the Son of God? Even after they assure you that it is Lazarus himself, you are curious about what it means. Rising from the dead is not self-explanatory.

These early Christian composers select words to express the specific meaning of the resurrection of this particular man, Jesus. John chooses a text of Scripture to affirm the importance of this event for all the chosen people: "Jesus is sitting at God's right hand."

It's like opening the office door in the morning, and there's a group of co-workers standing around listening to this young stranger tell jokes. You nod and go into your room. You can hear the laughter explode every so often.

In comes your secretary. "What was that all about?" you ask.

"Oh, that's the new CEO, Pendleton's nephew." Suddenly you are related to him in a very meaningful way.

The chosen people were now related to the ex-carpenter in a very meaningful way. He is now sitting at the right hand of the Lord himself. "All your hopes in the promises of God are being realized through Jesus."

8

The Second Coming

The Gospel is beginning to find expression. Words are being sought to clothe the mystery. Clothing a mystery with words can lead to dangers.

Like spotting the exotic bird deep in the forest, we use words to convey the glory we have seen. We are tempted to shift our attention from the inexpressible experience toward our ability to describe it, verbal formulas. "Now we do have it!"

We are tempted to control it, to hope that we can evoke the experience at will if we just use the right words, the correct incantation. It is the path to triumphalism: "We have the truth. It is ours." We lose sight of how little we believe it. This will always produce a betrayal of the Good News. It becomes something that "we can and do believe." Its essential incredibility is lost sight of.

The god has become a genie we can conjure up at will. But of course, the God we encountered has escaped us.

William Rose Benet pictures it vividly in his poem, "The Falconer of God." He has seen a "strange white heron with silver on its wings… crying wordless, wondrous things." And he sends up a falcon to capture this marvel. The falcon succeeds, but what it brings back is

> A dark and heavy weight
> Despoiled of silver plumage, its voice forever stilled,—
> All of the wonder
> Gone that ever filled
> Its guise with glory. Oh, bird that I have killed,
> How brilliantly you flew
> Across my rapturous vision when first I dreamed of you![9]

It was impossible for the disciples not to try to put into words the splendor they were encountering. How could they avoid killing the mystery as they wrapped it in words? Here is where the vivid awareness of their betrayal enabled the Apostles to say what had to be said: "How incredible we ourselves find it, even as we preach it! It is all too splendid to be true."

Even their memory of being given the mission to preach the Good News of the Kingdom brings to their mind the Risen Jesus reproaching them for their failure to believe. Only then did he commission them to preach—to preach what they didn't believe!

Like Leonard Bernstein's Credo from his *Mass*: assertions of "We believe" are interspersed with echoes: "We do not believe." The deeper the Apostles grasped the splendor, the more they experienced their unbelief. Jesus' death was *for* them and for their unbelief.

What fires the hearts of these early composers is so clear and so simple. It is the Christian *experience*. How can it mean so much to them? That extraordinary enthusiasm—how did it come to exist, and what happened to it? Didn't it soon fade out? Wasn't it built on the illusion that the end of the world was imminent? Wasn't its disappearance inevitable with the passage of time and the awareness that life goes on and on?

In getting at the experience of the earliest Christians we must find the deepest levels of their faith. We have seen throughout history the enthusiasm of millenarians, those who for one reason or another become convinced that the world is to end soon. Just as in the years AD 1000 and 2000, people expected remarkable, definitive events to occur.

When people who expect to be transformed into a new, glorious state of existence see their lives coming to a sudden end, there is often an unleashing of enthusiasm among them. Even though it is based on illusion, it has a powerful effect among those who believe. Earliest Christianity can be seen as merely a variation of this common pattern of illusion. The intense enthusiasm in which it grew and developed can appear to be the result of the illusory conviction that the Second Coming was imminent.

But this was not the case. This false expectation was, of course, present, but it was not central to their experience. Notice how in these earliest hymns the notion of a Second Coming is not present, and yet the core-gospel is expressed, and the reason for joy is spelled out.

There is indeed a proclaiming of the Second Coming in these early months. It can be no great surprise that the Apostolic band had misread the future in an overly optimistic way. As they come to tell of the history of their relationship with Jesus, the Apostles reveal themselves as having been filled with illusory hopes and quite incapable of hearing what Jesus was saying to them. Did he regret ever having told them they would sit on twelve thrones to judge the tribes of Israel? Those words they never forgot.

So, too, in the early months after the death of Jesus, the earliest disciples are convinced that the glorious coming of the kingdom is imminent. This does produce a release of emotions, but this is not what fired the joy of the disciples at its deepest level.

To get at the core experience of the first disciples, we must remember what their most recent personal history was. They are not people who had been leading ordinary lives and who were suddenly presented with a series of strange experiences: a man risen from the dead convinces them that their belief in his words will lead to great glory at the end-time.

We must get back into the story of these disciples as it actually happened to them. The man who appears to them after his death is a dear friend. They had abandoned him in his moment of greatest need. In fact, one of them had betrayed him to the authorities. Another, in fear for his own life, had denied that he had any part in him. These were men filled with guilt, and it is their guilt that must be included if we are to glimpse the dynamic that was operating among the earliest communities, and to explain their great joy. Their final acts of betrayal have been only the high point of a long pattern of refusing to understand and really listen to this marvelous man.

Now, guilt is a most peculiar experience. When we wrong someone, the feeling of guilt depends in part on the esteem we have for the person wronged. If I am slave to a brutal master, and I flee and take with me his money bank, I may feel no guilt at all. But if I get caught stealing from a most generous boss who had even been thinking of making me his heir, the guilt will be intense, even though the amount stolen may be rather small.

There can be an instance where I do not know the true value of a person—her kindnesses to me have been hidden. For instance: what if my neighbor is a woman who lives alone. Last November I had borrowed her rake, and I accidentally broke it. As spring comes, she tells me she can't find her rake, and asks whether I might still have it. I lie. I tell her I returned it months ago. She believes me. I don't feel good about it, of course, but...

Later I find out that this woman had lent my father a large sum of money when he was in an emergency and had no one else to turn to. The rule is: the more I learn of this person's true goodness, the greater my sense of guilt.

This is the situation the Apostles are in. These original Christians are filled with guilt at the crucifixion. But it is only the beginning. As they encounter the risen Lord, and become aware of who he is, their sense of guilt deepens. What is it like to realize that the man who has befriended you is God's own Son, and you had failed him so miserably? It is easy to forget the nature of the dynamics of forgiveness and to concentrate only on the joy element of the earliest Church. The experience of guilt does not go away when someone finds forgiveness. It remains and inevitably deepens, but it is no longer alone. Now it is part of a larger complex of which joy is the major note.

Peter felt guilty the minute he denied the Lord, and knew he had done wrong. But it was only in the experience of being forgiven that his guilt fully flowered. That is the nature of being forgiven. That profound guilt-experience is fundamental to the development of the Early Church.

This is at the core of the spirituality of the earliest communities—a pervasive sense of guilt. It meant that we find only one spirituality in these first days. The Paschal experience is too vivid for the temptation to humanize Jesus' teachings to get a foothold. That will come soon enough.

Just as triumphalism plays no part in their daily life, neither does any effort to qualify the unique focus on God's gifts and his actions. The Pelagian impulse will appear soon enough to muddy the waters. The reluctance to lead people into their sinfulness and guilt is waiting in the wings.

For the first disciples the experience of being forgiven is the heart of their life with God and the energy source of their apostolate. It will persist in the Church, but it will be forced to compete with more "reasonable" paths to joy that stress human effort rather than divine gifts, and striving to be worthy, and the willingness to run your best race and win the prize. The fear of "cheap grace" will produce the demand for a spirituality calling for heroism.

Paganism's defenders will treat with contempt Christianity's formula summoning people to her mysteries: "Whoever is a sinner, whoever is unwise, whoever is a child, and whoever is a wretch... welcome!" But this call would have been eagerly heard by the Apostles. And the invitation to the pagan mysteries—"Whosoever has pure hands and a wise tongue..."—would have turned them away.[10]

The earliest disciples' guilt affects their thinking and their preaching. It comes through as they proclaim the gospel. It raises an echo in the hearts of certain listeners. The good news is a call to believe in a wonderful goodness and an awful truth, at one and the same time.

Only someone who is open to the full message will be drawn to true belief. The Apostles invite their hearers to share their guilt, and *thereby* enter into their experience of forgiveness and joy.

So, Peter makes that little addition: Jesus has suffered once "for all," the righteous for the unrighteous. The sense of being the unrighteous that the Apostles carry through life infects others and becomes the vehicle for their sharing in resurrection joy. Especially is this felt at the Lord's Supper. For the Apostles to hear again the words of Jesus, so fresh in their memories but now filled with new meanings coming from the events of the last few months—it is hard to imagine the impact of such a ritual.

Everything is subject to Jesus, and he intercedes for them at God's right hand. They are singing about the heart of the good news, that complex of guilt and forgiveness that the Jesus-Event means for them.

Far from being a quaint form of gospel expression and one that was spoiled by a Second Coming illusion, these songs are quite precise in their presentation of what was to become the permanent gospel. The guilt experience communicated in the preaching leads to the spontaneous rise of prophecies and admonitions at the liturgies, elements that have the most striking effects on the hearts of the listeners. In the preaching of true guilt the Apostles and the earliest disciples are preaching a pattern of life that is appropriate for those who have been freely forgiven. It is what we see in the lives of the saints.

The expectation of an imminent Second Coming is indeed present and important but it is not at the heart of the Apostles' experience nor of their preaching. That involves a much deeper level of reality, where they are forgiven and restored to friendship by that very death in which they had played such a shameful part.

These earliest hymns are the creations of the Hebraist synagogue. Their content is primitive, as we have seen. They affirm the death of Jesus and its importance for all. Then they proclaim the resurrection. To these two narrative statements is added a phrase to interpret the meaning of the resurrection: it is enthronement of Jesus at God's right hand. Then a few verses from Psalm 8 spell out the present power of Jesus.

Very little is present in these hymns other than the barest bones of the gospel. It is just enough to explain why this Jesus is being given the cultic veneration that had been up to now considered appropriate only for God himself.

The hymns serve as much more than just songs. Since they are the opportunity for the creative spirits to express the newness of the Jesus-Event in a new way, they become most effective teaching instruments. They contain a basic creed. "This is what we believe." The message of the gospel finds its clear expression in these new songs. The preachers quote them in their sermons and exhortations. It is the way the earliest communities share their faith. Before the development of a creed and any statement of common belief, the hymns play that role. They are the first channel for the developing thinking of the early Church.

In writing the hymns, people have an outlet for their reflections on the Jesus-Event. In singing them the community is invited to echo their interpretations of the event. It is a golden age in which the theologians write the hymns and the congregations get to respond at once, and their responses are heard. Some of the hymns are very short-lived, for they find little resonance in the devotion of the group. But many are welcomed and they are used constantly and gradually become sacred texts.

What a strange development: hymns playing a crucial role in the early Church. It flows from the unexpected decision of Jesus to ritualize his death. His deliberate invitation to grasp the full meaning of his life and death in the breaking of the bread inevitably leads to a ritual which does not yet have a full script. It is a new kind of coming together. It inevitably produces new forms.

During these earliest days there is a vast experienced meaningfulness that is searching for expression. The weight of the spectacular glory of the good news presses forward to be put into words. Brand new, never-before-used phrases are being invented and tried out. The boundaries of the significance of the event are not clear—if there are any at all!

Let us take it step by step, to get the full flavor of this earliest period, and what it was like to be part of those first communities.

9

Who Do You Say I Am?

In those earliest days in the Temple the disciples preached the Good News. When they spoke of Jesus, he was portrayed as the one who had revealed the Good News. But at first there was no sharp focus on the nature of his inner reality, but rather on his mission to save Israel from the impending doom, his opening up of a path to salvation. This was in line with Jesus' own emphasis on how to get people to tap into the powers of the kingdom, the New Age that was coming in. In the recollections of the Apostles Jesus did not focus on his own identity. He preached that the power of God was being given away and those who were willing to receive it would be filled with joy.

This is what nowadays we would call a spirituality. I once heard a spiritual problem defined as a problem which is solved by the coming of the Spirit. Jesus had focused on our need for faith and love, and permanent joy. Jesus centered his preaching on the promise of a conquest of death itself. Such was the kingdom and the power of the gifts of the Spirit now unleashed upon the world.

There was a spectacular newness about it. Like the transition from horse-power to gasoline power that caught everyone's attention around the turn of the last century, the new energy source—the Spirit—required a "know-how." The Apostles, like Jesus before them, concentrated at first on that "How-To" question, the spirituality question. Just as harness-makers and blacksmiths began to disappear with the coming of the gasoline engine, and most people no longer learned how to ride a horse, so too the new wine of the Good News outmoded many old wineskins.

The new preaching featured the Love-Command and humility,

the experience of guilt and being forgiven, and a new kind of faith that neither demanded nor needed signs.

That was the most striking break with the tradition. In the covenant enshrined in the Scriptures that the disciples had heard all their lives, there was a very clear description of a faith that rested on signs. Even Abraham asked God for a sign to help him believe in the Lord's promises, and God produced a miraculous smoking firepot and a flaming torch moving between two rows of slaughtered animals in the dark (Genesis 15:8).

Later in the time of the Judges, Gideon also asked for signs and got them. Receiving the divine commission to save Israel from Midianite oppression, Gideon says, "If you look on me with favor, give me a sign that you are the one speaking with me." So a miraculous fire consumes his offering. Later he asks God to bring it about that, "If indeed you are going to save Israel through me, as you have said, I am putting this woolen fleece on the threshing-floor, and if dew is on the fleece alone, while all the ground is dry, I shall know that you will save Israel through me, as you have said." And that happened.

Then Gideon asks God not to get angry with his next request. This time Gideon asks that by morning the fleece be dry and the ground wet. And God does that (Judges 6:11-40).

In the time of the kings, Hezekiah was given a sign: after God promised to add fifteen years to his life, he had the sun's shadow falling on a staircase go back ten steps (Isaiah 38:1-6, 7-8, 21-22).

But as the Apostles recalled very vividly, Jesus had been angered at people who asked for signs. One of the disciples recounted that day when Jesus "sighed from the depth of his spirit and said, 'Why does this generation seek a sign?'" (Mark 8:12).

On another occasion they recalled how he had labeled sign-seekers as an "evil and adulterous generation" (Matthew 12:39).

There was a fatal inadequacy in sign-faith, and it went to the difference between the promises of the covenant with Israel, and the promises Jesus had made. The fulfillment of the promises of the covenant with Israel took place in a way obvious to all. Land, children, and a long life—these are either given and quite perceptible before you die, or the promises are unfulfilled. But Jesus had shifted to promising the imperceptible gift of the Spirit, and the after-death gift of eternal life. The faith Jesus demanded of his followers had to come before any signs of fulfillment.

So often, after working a miracle, Jesus mentioned the vital role of faith. To the woman cured of the hemorrhage, "Your faith has saved you" (Matthew 9:22). To the blind men, and the centurion, "Let it be done for you according to your faith" (Matthew 9:28, 8:13). Even the forgiveness of sin rests on a previous act of faith: to the woman known as sinful, "Your faith has saved you" (Luke 7:36-50). To the grateful leper Jesus says, "Your faith has saved you" (Luke 17:19).

It's as if Jesus realized the threat posed by his working miracles. They would produce a sign-faith, and that would not be enough to enter the kingdom.

One of the disciples tells of an occasion when they were all happy after a very successful mission. But Jesus stopped them. "Do not rejoice in this." He then pointed out the invisible source of a true believer's joy: "Your names are written in heaven" (Luke 10:17-20).

The growth of sign-faith is produced by a simple dynamic, one we are familiar with from everyday life: someone reveals a pattern of trustworthy behavior and we trust them.

But where does this new kind of faith come from? It is a sharing in the divine consciousness, a knowing the heart of God that can come only with the coming of the Spirit. It is given freely to those who ask for it. It is at the core of the coming of the kingdom.

It is the gift which would have enabled the Apostles to be present at Calvary when there were no signs at all. But they had been so confident they had abundant faith that Jesus' words had no impact on them until after his death.

Their sign-faith would feel strong when they worked miracles, and very weak when their boat was in the storm. The roller-coaster of ups and downs produced no lasting joy, and their inner assurance and their decisions were governed by the presence or absence of signs. In Jeremiah God said: "Am I a God near at hand only, and not a God far off?" (Jeremiah 23:23).

The entry into the kingdom was through the gift of the Spirit: a faith that neither asked nor needed signs, a faith that ignored appearances in its decision to believe—no matter how bad things may seem.

In the earliest months after the resurrection of Jesus the disciples preach the same message with its focus on how to avoid the wrath to come, and how to enter into exaltation. But soon a separate focus begins to draw their attention: "Who is this man that *his* death can be *for all*?"

During Jesus' public years he preached his "spirituality"—"with authority." Eventually the question was raised, "By what authority do you do this?" His personal identity gradually became of central importance.

The same shift of focus occurs for the earliest disciples. Little by little the question of Jesus' identity pushes itself into the foreground. Their efforts to respond to that question led to a rapidity of christological development that will never occur again. Never again would Christianity be so heavy on experience and so thin on precise verbal expression. A vocabulary is invented in just a few years. One of the main accomplishments of these early disciples is discovering the phrases that clothe the mystery comfortably.

It is not easy for us to imagine the scene. Nowadays we are a-swim in verbal formulas. No issue that arises is without a great mass of rather precise vocabulary that has a history spelling out its meaning. We are like a modern auto plant where each part, no matter how spontaneous it may look, has been formed in a carefully made mold. These earliest preachers have to handtool every item. One of the commentators has used a most apt phrase: "the exegetical workshop of the early Church." More development takes place within that first decade than was to occur over many centuries to come.

We do have a parallel that may help us in post-USSR Russia. The molds have been broken, and new elements are being handcrafted. Parts of the old structures are still in place, and sometimes the new item does not fit well with the old, and what you get is worse than what you had before. Adjustments are constantly being made, tried out, rejected, or modified. Occasionally there is a wonderful success. A new item is quite effective and it catches on. But even more often the new effort is quickly seen to be useless and is abandoned.

So it is during the first decade of Christianity. Phrases that seem very promising often prove of little use. Some traditional phrases are given a slight twist, and prove most effective. At times a new phrase is tried out and found successful and it becomes embedded in the new tradition.

What are the bare bones? Jesus had died and had, afterward, appeared to his followers. Of themselves, these bare bones have no specific meaning at all. Were I to tell you that my Uncle Tom had died, and that afterward he had appeared to his brother, and then showed up at a big family reunion where he was seen by quite a few of the guests—even if you did believe me—what meaning would it have?

If he warned the guests not to eat the fettuccine, there would be a lot of leftover fettuccine. But notice: it would not suggest to anyone who saw him that he was divine. These bare bones—that he died and had risen—of themselves say nothing. They get their meaning from the life of the person who has died, and from his words as he appears after death.

In other words, the meaning of these two events comes to the early disciples from what Jesus had said about them. It is Jesus' own claim about the significance of his life that is the foundation stone of the meaning of this particular man's resurrection. When Lazarus was raised from the dead, there was no suggestion that his resurrection signified anything concerning his personal dignity. He didn't say anything about the meaning of his being raised. His resurrection took its meaning from Jesus' words. But Jesus had spoken about the meaning of his own rising from the dead.

Most vivid in the memory of the disciples is that Jesus had spoken of the imminent coming of the kingdom. God is about to intervene in human history and save his people. There is a wrath that is coming and there is an escape route available. God is about to step in and save his chosen ones in an unprecedented way.

Jesus has made these promises and Jesus has risen. The meaning is clear: the salvation he promised is at hand.

A task is now accepted by the disciples: spread the glorious news to all of Israel. The moment when all is going to happen has arrived. His resurrection shows that Jesus had been right after all. He is God's instrument for the salvation of his people. God is using Jesus to offer an escape route. His death has not been the failure of God's plan. It is somehow a critical part of it. His death has to be preached, too. It is itself a part of the good news.

That's what the rising of this particular man means. Because of what he had preached during his lifetime, Jesus' resurrection means that his preaching is true, and his promises and warnings are about to be realized. He is indeed as he claimed to be, the center of human history, and the coming to completion of God's plan to save his people.

Once you get into the "how" of salvation, especially when this "how" involves as an essential element the death of the savior, then it becomes inevitable that the question of the savior's identity will be raised. Anyone who can produce salvation by dying has to be of extraordinary stature.

But, in the earliest days, the resurrection is a sign of the fulfillment of the promises of salvation. Its first meaning is that forgiveness is assured to all. The deliverance from sin that had been promised is now on the scene. Sin, and its unbearable companion, guilt, and its inevitable result, death—these threats have been triumphed over. An escape route has been opened up. The word must be spread abroad.

During Jesus' public ministry the Apostles had been waiting eagerly for the day when he would send them out to preach. They daydreamed the scenario many times: first, there would be some revelation of power; the carpenter of Nazareth shows himself to be the long awaited Messiah. A string of spectacular miracles establishes his authority. He feeds thousands at a sitting. The crowds grow rapidly. He calms the stormy sea with a gesture. He turns their water into wine. He points out where to put their nets down to catch boatloads of fish. He heals the sick, and he begins to raise the dead.

Then he would start for Jerusalem with immense crowds following him. He sends his disciples out as heralds of the good news. They are miraculously protected from poisons, snakes, and every danger. They enter the villages and announce the good news. Where they meet rejection, they shake the dust from their feet, and walk away from a doomed people. It was wonderful to daydream about.

How eager the disciples had been to get it all started. Perhaps the dream comes to a climax with Jesus standing on the pinnacle of the Temple in full view of the great festival crowds. He steps off into space. Suddenly the sky is filled with angels who would bring him safely to earth.

But their daydreams come to a swift end. Instead the Messiah never opens his mouth. He is led to be slaughtered and he goes like a lamb. Like a dumb sheep, he never opens his mouth (Isaiah 53:7).

Despite this catastrophic change of script, the disciples still see the risen Jesus in a role that is without parallel. To be at his Supper Table is to taste the salvation of God. Remembering his death in ritual is the fullest proclamation of God's startling intervention. The Lord's Supper does not become a minor devotional practice added to the Temple worship and the synagogue service.

While the phrase that will pinpoint exactly who Jesus is has not yet been formulated, the message being preached in the Temple is quite clear. A parting of the ways is at hand. Doom threatens but there is an escape route. "Where is it? What must we do to get on it?" Peter replies: "Repent!"

Forgiveness is available and the source of the forgiveness is Jesus himself.

As they stand up to preach forgiveness in the Temple, they raise in people's minds the other question: "Who is this Jesus?" This question leads the disciple to search for phrases that will identify Jesus. The preachers begin to search for a title that will capture his exact status. They are seeking diamonds and the fields they work in are the Scriptures. There is a copy of the Law and the Prophets in their synagogue, and it is often in use. The disciples have large parts of it memorized, but in their eagerness to get their message across to the Israelite people, they now go through the texts most carefully.

One afternoon Peter chances upon a vision in the Book of Daniel:

> In the vision I saw during the night,...
> I saw coming with the clouds of heaven
> one like a son of man.
> When he reached the Ancient of Days
> and was presented before him,
> he received dominion, splendor, and kingship;
> all nations, peoples, and tongues will serve him.
> His dominion is an everlasting dominion

> that shall not pass away,
> his kingship, one that shall not be destroyed.
> —Daniel 7:13-14

The voice of Jesus echoes in Peter's memory. How often Jesus had used that phrase: "son of man." Jesus liked to refer to himself that way.

The next day Peter uses it in his Temple preaching. "Fellow Israelites, this is what has just happened in the heavens! As God was raising Jesus from the dead here in this city, in the heavens he was enthroning Jesus at his own right hand." God has chosen a viceroy!

This was the backdrop against which human history, and each individual human life, was being played out. The heart of God had been revealed, laid bare: each person was made in order to be adopted into the Godhead.

Such was Jesus who had projected himself as the center of human history, the universal messiah whose choices were decisive for everyone. That was the Jesus the Apostles described at the suppers. That was what they now believed about him: he had been sent, and they too had been sent.

It is like in a sci-fi film of a squalid village on a planet far from anywhere, completely apart from "where the action is." But in the next scene we are at the heart of the galaxy, in the very control room. There the cabinet discusses those mud-dwellers with obvious concern. Their fate is of great concern to the Emperor himself.

This is the kind of faith Jesus demands: choose for the backdrop to your sleeping and rising one of unlimited meaningfulness. That is what the Apostles saw Jesus choosing, and inviting them to choose.

John Bowker writes, "in jargonistic language, but language which does justice to the evidence which has survived in the Gospels,"

> Jesus gave the impression of existing in an information net of stable communication with a reality external to himself which he characterized theistically (as Abba, Father), and of then extending the information net to include others. So unequivocally powerful was the consequent *dunamis* of the-

> istic input into the construction of life that it led, not simply to the transformation of life, but in a more dramatic word, to its transfiguration (Mk 9:2 ff.).[11]

They chose to project themselves as the leaders of an expedition which had begun to head for home. They were hoping to lead as many as would trust them, saving them from the sea of meaningless life and death that threatened them.

They projected a backdrop in which they were chosen by the central human will, the human will whose choices were the focal point of the human story. Their Lord had come from the heart of the real. He had descended into the deepest unreality, and uttered a call—and his sheep scattered over the hillsides would hear his voice.

The visionary Maeve in H. F. M. Prescott's *The Man on a Donkey*:

> So is the triumph of that High One
> great and peaceable, homely and glorious,
> and now and forever He sitteth down to His feast,
> waiting till we sit down with Him,
> and all the children have come home.
> But it is He Himself who bringeth us,
> each one upon His shoulder.
> We have but to stay still until He lift and carry us.[12]

The appearances of Jesus after his death are but the outer shell of a stupendous event that has occurred in the heavens. An event in God has taken place: the vision of Daniel has been enacted in the heavenly court. In the heavens, Jesus was led into the presence of the One most venerable, and on him was bestowed authority over all.

This title, "Son of Man," is one of the first the Apostles use, the one Jesus himself had selected.

But the title the Apostles turn to most often is the one Jesus avoided, "Messiah" or "Christ." Its literal meaning is "the anointed one."

This title "Messiah" had not been of much use to Jesus in explaining his mission. It was loaded down with elements of earthly rule that were not part of his image of himself. Nevertheless it clings to him. What he did claim for himself, that final and central role in the coming of the kingdom, forces people to turn to the most popular image in the tradition, the Messiah, the Anointed One. Even his death is linked with the messianic expectations he had aroused. It is no great step when the disciples begin to use the title of him after the resurrection. When they find in Psalm 2 God saying; "I myself have anointed my king" (verse 6), they apply it easily to Jesus.

He is the anointed one, the Christ, because he fulfills the promises of Scripture. All of Scripture has become a sign pointing directly at Jesus. Everything that had been written up to now is just an arrow. That conviction is behind the use of the term "Messiah" by the early disciples.

To produce a desired effect, a poet will compare his beloved's eyes to something else. "They are as blue as April skies." But this image has been used so often that it doesn't work anymore on those who have read much. It is so worn out it doesn't register in the imagination.

To avoid the trite, the poet searches for the untried, the new. Now the danger is that he will come up with something so unusual that very few of the readers, if any, will see the connection intended. "Her eyes were like cracked ice."

In using "Son of Man" Jesus was struggling to find a way of explaining his identity without confusing it with any political champion. The Apostles now find that Jesus had reached too far. He had come up with an image, "Son of Man," that needs endless explanation.

But "Christ" is a success. It is a claim of great dignity for Jesus, and the people readily get the message.

Since Jesus is the one who leads everyone to safety along an escape route that he has opened up, why don't the Apostles call him savior? It will eventually become one of his most common titles.

But in these earliest days, the title "Savior" is not really available. Its use had been largely restricted to God alone. Except for some of the judges of early Israel (Judges 3-9), it had never been used as a *title* for any human figure the way "Anointed" has been. Nor is it linked to any particular salvation. It has only a general reference as when we say, "I had a flat. Fortunately along came a savior in the person of an elderly man." "Savior" was not a title linked to the one who was to come.

What did Jesus do? He saved. But the noun has no more specific reference than that. A savior is anyone who saves. Unlike "Messiah" and "Son of Man" with their links to the end-time, "savior" has only a general meaning. It begins to come forward and be used frequently of Jesus only many decades later.

Who is Jesus? He is the Christ. He is the Son of Man. The mystery within him which the disciples have touched is still struggling to be uttered. But in the beginning this process of defining Jesus—naming him—is not a central preoccupation. It moves forward clumsily, and not in a straight line. It takes a secondary place to the preaching, and the preaching centers on what Jesus had done and what Israel must do. For those disciples who get involved in composing the hymns, the question of naming Jesus keeps coming up. They search for the "best word." Step by step they start to sketch in the lines of the Jesus-phenomenon.

Reading Scripture scholars on the early Church is something like listening to the relatives as they stand around the first "showing" of the new baby.

"Those are definitely his mama's eyes."

"But where did he get that beautiful blonde hair? Nobody in our family is blonde."

"Grandma's sister Ellen had long blonde hair."

"Jesus preached the kingdom, but out came the Church!"

Every feature of the new reality is traced back to its origins. If there's something that Jesus emphasized in his preaching, and it doesn't seem to be in the early Church, that cries out for an explanation.

"Paul must have been the father!" Or the pagan converts, or John the Presbyter, or the Essenes, or the mystery religions.

How odd that the liturgy played such a major role in the early Church and yet it was barely mentioned in the Apostles' recollections of Jesus.

They do fill their mealtimes with storytelling, some of them miraculous, but the Apostles don't recount any explicit instruction on what was to be so central a part of their future. He had laid the foundations for an effective Eucharistic experience very carefully:

the Love-Command, humility, the kingdom of God bringing forgiveness through him, and a most intimate union with him.

Without the womb of Eucharistic fellowship would the earliest disciples have ever come to know who they really were? These gatherings involved them in experiencing Jesus in a very particular way. He was encountered as the transcendent one, the one who forgives all their sins and who releases the power of the New Age, the Spirit. The disciples were drawn into a pattern of continuing to encounter the Risen Lord in his full paschal reality, the One through whom and in whom all the promises are realized.

Before long the Early Christians do get into christology, trying to identify fully the person of Jesus. But this had never been a central emphasis for Jesus as the Apostles remember him. He preached the kingdom rather than the messiah.

The Kingdom of God was coming in, an age of extraordinary gifts. A new power was becoming available, a new energy-source. Jesus was intent on teaching people how to tap into this new energy-source, the Spirit of God.

His attention was riveted on that new power. What he saw in Israel was a very critical scene, and he knew the Father's determination to save his Chosen People. He wanted people to become familiar with the choices they could make that would unite their wills to the mighty flow of divine action. By opening themselves to the gifts of the Spirit, they would grow in their love for others, and their joy would abound.

Jesus was involved in spelling out the "How-To" of the New Age. This was his spirituality: how to tap the flow of divine energy. He taught them how vital honesty was, and how it led to being exalted, to living in the fullness of the Kingdom of God.

Much of his preaching was an effort to wake people up to the enormous consequences their present choices entail: eternal life with God, or eternal pain in the darkness outside. He preached as the prophets had before him.

> On Zion sinners are in dread,
> trembling grips the impious;
> 'Who of us can live with the consuming fire?
> Who of us can live with the everlasting flames?'
> —Isaiah 33:13-14

In his eyes this was a generation challenged by a most fateful decision. All past history had been looking forward to this moment. God was about to intervene and save his people. An incredible glory was at hand.

Let the sea and all within it thunder;
the world, and all its peoples.
Let the rivers clap their hands
and the hills ring out their joy.
Rejoice at the presence of the Lord,
for he comes to rule the earth.
He will rule the world with justice
and the peoples with fairness.
—Psalm 98:7-9

10

Time Bombs

What may have been the outcome had the titles "Messiah" and "Son of Man" proved to be all that the disciples needed? Would the search to identify Jesus have ended there? The rapid development in christology might have come to a halt. The disciples might have closed down the exegetical workshop.

But though the disciples find the two titles useful, they still feel that much of Jesus' identity is being left out. The search goes on.

The next step proves to be a major advance in expressing their faith. It comes out of the Psalms that are used each day by the Temple preachers, and that are sung occasionally at the suppers.

The first texts of the new faith are Psalms 2 and 110. Christian exegesis begins there. Its earliest expression, "Jesus is enthroned," comes from these two texts.

In hearing these Psalms, some of the disciples recall to mind the peculiar way Jesus prayed. He used the word *'abba* for God. This is the ordinary name a child uses for his father. To call God by this name is a practice uncommon for the Jews of Jesus' day. But his followers cannot forget his voice as he used this word in prayer. This is an important part of their knowing Jesus. Here is a striking peculiarity of his, one that they knew spoke worlds about his inner self.

Now as they listen to Psalm 2, they notice this phrase:

> God said to me, 'You are my son;
> Today I have begotten you.'
> — Psalm 2:7

And as they listen to Psalm 110, they hear this phrase:

From the womb, before the dawn, I begot you.
— Psalm 110:3

Jesus had prayed as if he was God's son in a special way. This conviction of his now germinates in the reflections of the early disciples.

It finds its way into the preaching in the Temple. It is expressed in careful statements, some of which are more successful than others. The successful ones catch on. Here is one of the earliest successes. It is later quoted by Paul at the beginning of his Letter to the Romans.

Jesus is descended from David
according to the flesh;
Jesus has been appointed son of God
by the resurrection of the dead.
— Romans 1:3-4

The two facts of death and resurrection are there. But the focus has shifted to the dignity of Jesus as son of God.

Traditionally the phrase "son of God" has been commonly used in a number of ways. It has been applied to the suffering righteous man, and to the wise man. It can mean very little.

But it can mean much more. It is a most happy phrase for the Church because it has great potential. It leaves room for development, for further precision as the faith of the believers clarifies.

The two elements, "son of David" and "son of God," are both present in the Nathan prophecy also.

I will raise up your offspring after you,
sprung from your loins,
I will be a father to him and he shall be a son to me.
— 2 Samuel 7:12, 14

This is how it works. The disciples are in a state of high receptivity to certain possible messages. They are tuned to welcoming certain suggestions. A particular text will suggest something. One of the disciples picks it up. A second text echoes it. In his next preaching, he puts the two together. One of the disciples who hears him is reminded of a third text that says almost the same thing, and maybe a little bit more. Scripture is being heard in a new way. Scripture's heart is being revealed.

In this "exegetical workshop of the early Church," the fundamental building blocks are being put in place. First one combination is tried out, then another. It is not the central work of the community. It is rather a secondary affair, taking place haphazardly, much as with the writing of the hymns. The preaching and the baptizing, the services and the Lord's Supper, these are the center of the life of the early congregations. Writing hymns and creating formulas of faith are done as a person feels inspired in the times between. But that small part of their day is nurturing a reflective impulse that will grow and grow.

In human history it often happens that a small group of enthusiasts takes a path that guarantees a limited audience. For example, a specific date is set for the end of the world. When that doesn't occur, the group loses identity and scatters. This is not the case with Jesus' followers. Hidden within the bosom of this small community, certain close followers of Jesus are learning how to express an incredible message for the world. It will find a receptive audience in every generation and touches hearts even in our day.

But it begins here:

> Jesus is the son of David
> according to the flesh;
> Jesus has been appointed son of God
> by the resurrection of the dead.
> —Romans 1:3-4

Notice how in this formula Jesus is seen as becoming God's son through his resurrection. The attention is on the meaning of the resurrection. What does it mean that Jesus is again alive? It means that he is the fulfillment of Nathan's prophecy, that he is God's son in a special way—"God's Son." But in the process of explicating the meaning of the resurrection, it presents Jesus as becoming "God's

Son" only at his resurrection. Soon this suggestion is going to be discarded. It is overtaken by other phrases created later, that the community will find more comfortable. But at the time it is made up and first used, it is seen as an excellent affirmation of who Jesus is.

In using it, the congregation is invited to react: what did you think of it? The Hebraist disciple who wrote it in Aramaic is delighted at the people's response, especially when one of the bilinguists translates it for the Hellenist synagogue. It is only after other formulas are created that people notice the inadequacies present in this one. But before that occurs, it has become so popular that it has achieved a certain place of honor.

Here is another very early formula of faith. It is found in Peter's preaching in the Acts of the Apostles.

> He is now raised to the heights
> by God's right hand.
> For David himself never went up to heaven,
> but yet he said,
> 'The LORD declared to my Lord,
> "Take your seat at my right hand."'
> Jesus was crucified.
> Now God has made him Lord and Christ.
> —Cf. Acts 2:33-36

Here the exegetical process is very easy to see. There is a sacred text, a prophecy. But that prophecy has never been fulfilled. The resurrection of Jesus means that this prophecy is now fulfilled in Jesus. This way of using the prophecies became a common pattern in the early Church.

Present also in this formula is the phrase, "Lord." It comes from the daily liturgical use of the early congregations: "Jesus is Lord." What they had called Jesus during his life on earth is still being used: "Lord." It is an easy transition. In fact, how could it be otherwise?

But there is present in the ambiguities of that title seeds of endless possible growth. Under the influence of Psalm 110, the title "Lord" will take on much of the richer meaning that the disciples now find in the risen Jesus. They use it in worship and in private prayer. As a form of direct address it comes to be used in the formulas of belief, and, in the process, takes on even more meaning.

This title of reverence that originally expresses their personal relationship with the risen Jesus comes to suggest that Jesus is of a dignity that has previously been reserved to God alone.

Because "Lord" is the common title for God himself, it puts no limit on the dignity that Jesus may have in his risen existence. It does not spell out its unbounded possibility, but it leaves it open, as an invitation. Later the Church will accept this invitation.

It is not easy for us to grasp the touch of the absurd that is present in the preaching of this good news. We have become so familiar with the image of a God who dies that it has become worn out. It has no shock value. To recapture something of the original experience, we must labor, just as we do when we try to relive Newton's shock at the discovery of gravity's laws.

To elevate someone long dead to the level of the superhuman is easier to understand. In tribal memory banks, the earliest heroes take on more-than-human proportions, and are often seen as direct descendants of the gods. The passage of the years blurs the sharp details of the fully human figure, and a radiance fills out the empty space where before there had been wrinkles and sweat and liver spots.

But the earliest disciples of Jesus are putting a halo around a head they had seen to be thoroughly human only a few months before.

Distance can also blur the humanity of an emperor. His rare appearances are staged to be godlike. The public never sees him vomit or hiccup. His fevers are visible to very few. Only a close circle get near him. His image is being crafted for divinization. But the disciples had been close enough to touch Jesus. They had seen him eat and sweat, wash and sleep and sneeze. They had seen him filled with fear. They had seen him bleed.

Often we find that knowing a person intimately brings us into touch with their basic animality. This can disappear with the passage of time or by the carefully selected moments of imperial appearances. "Familiarity breeds contempt." No man is a hero to his valet.

In Thornton Wilder's *Our Town*, as Doctor Gibbs muses on his fine son's forthcoming marriage, he sounds that very familiar note: "Ye-e-es! I get a shock every time I think of George setting out to be a family man—that great gangling thing!"[13]

Our image of those we live with day after day is filled with their animality, their humanity, their weakness. It is not easy to read anything superhuman into anyone with whom we share a bathroom.

How could the disciples have come to see Jesus in this more than human role after living with him in such close quarters, and within months of his disgrace?

There is another level of the incredible in this rapid elevation of Jesus. The disciples had become so familiar with Jesus that they had reached the point of ignoring much of what he said! As we do so often with those with whom we live, they had learned when and how to turn him off.

In fact, his greatest concerns were often ignored. The deepest level of his inner life was brushed aside. His most profound conviction—that his death would be salvation for others—was thoroughly ignored. As often happens within a family, Jesus made spectacular efforts to get through their reluctance to hear him, and failed.

Ironically, this ignored element was to play a major role in providing the superhuman detail that filled their post-resurrection image of Jesus. He is now Lord and Christ.

Perhaps the earliest book of the New Testament is Paul's Letter to the Thessalonians. Here is a formula he uses in that very First Letter.

> We are now servants of the living and true God,
> who raised his son Jesus from the dead.
> We are waiting for Jesus to come from heaven.
> Jesus will save us from the coming wrath.
> —Cf. 1 Thessalonians 1:9-10

Had the disciples simply repeated his teachings and presented him as a wise man, and focused on the truth of what he had preached, his death could have been relegated to the level of a nonessential anecdote. But the resurrection is being preached as the heart of the message, and the death of Jesus is brought front and center, and demands an explanation. Their conviction that his dying is at the center of the Good News impels them to find out precisely how this can be so.

The awareness of his coming death had forced Jesus himself to face the question: Who must I be that I shall save the people by dying? Now the disciples will follow in his footsteps. Who is this Jesus? Who must he be that he can save Israel by his dying?

The early disciples are choosing. They are making decisions. We may see it as an inevitable development without any realistic alternatives. But they are choosing—accepting and rejecting the suggestions that come to them.

What is the dynamic at work as they seek words for a sermon or a song? How do you decide to accept or reject a phrase you hear for the first time at the supper-ritual?

Properly deciding involves us in discernment, a process that has attracted great interest in our day. A most effective way of choosing is based on happiness. A choice is effective if it leads to greater happiness than its alternative. But we do not see the future. How can we tell beforehand which alternative will lead to greater happiness in the long run?

We must seek the richest level of happiness already present within ourselves. It will be seen as related to a pattern of choices. The new choice will be felt as in harmony with that pattern or as contrary to it.

In Christianity this deepest level is the joy of experiencing God. What happens when a suggestion comes to me? Does it prove a welcome companion to my experience of joy in God's presence? Or does it trouble this deepest peace?

Now the spiritual tradition does caution us: this peace and joy must be authentic to be of any use as a criterion of future choices. It must be a joy received as a surprise, and not as the result of techniques of prayer. We can at times hypnotize ourselves into a sense of peace: "Every day in every way I am getting better and better." The resulting peace is nothing but the product of my own efforts. It will be a most deceptive criterion. It lacks the reality that accompanied the gift of peace.

For the Christian the happiness level that is sought is an assurance of God's forgiving love that comes into the heart. The path to this experience obviously goes through a realistic sense of sinfulness. Into the midst of a deeply felt need to be forgiven comes an awareness of being forgiven.

The risen Jesus had assured the disciples he had forgiven their cowardice. Their failures do not lessen his desire for their friendship. One very clear effect of their experience of being forgiven is their hesitation to throw their weight around. Great prestige is theirs but they are reluctant to use it. It could be said that they do not see themselves as the ones to make the decisions. When a title is used with a new meaning, they do not rush to judgment. Everyone gets heard.

The joy of the disciples at Jesus' kindly restoration of friendship becomes the criterion of their choices. What can be placed next to that joy without discomfort is accepted. What troubles it, is rejected.

They had seen this dynamic at work in Jesus also. But in his case it was not an awareness of being forgiven. The new community considers those who had been present with Jesus from his baptism on to be special witnesses. There in the Jordan Jesus had chosen to identify himself with his sinful brothers and sisters. That choice, accompanied by great consolations, was the visible beginning of a pattern of choices that led him to his deliberate surrender to being put to death "for all."

The earliest disciples are making choices based on their experience of God in Jesus. In many cases, the consequences of the choice have not been thought through. But at the moment of decision, it is found to fit their joy in the Lord, and that is enough for them to go on.

Some patterns have taken on definite form within a few weeks. Introducing the new converts to the supper-ritual requires a minimal instruction in what is happening and why—how it is due to a command of Jesus himself.

This we received from the Lord.

On the night he was betrayed, he took some bread,
gave thanks,
broke it, and said,
'This is my flesh for the life of the world.
Do this in remembrance of me.'
—Cf. 1 Corinthians 11:23

The rite forces the disciples to focus on the death of Jesus. It guarantees that the Good News will always include that shameful death.

Perhaps we have here the beginning of that sense which surfaces in Christianity regularly: only the absurd is believable. Were what is preached credible, could it possibly flow from a divine intervention? Doesn't credibility imply a certain plausibility that, while it makes it more understandable, also makes it unlikely that it involves a superhuman origin beyond our imagining?

Joseph Ratzinger states the paradox well in his *Introduction to Christianity*:

> God is the quite other, invisible, unrecognizable.
> But when he really did appear upon the scene,
> so other,
> so invisible in regard to his divinity,
> so unrecognizable,
> it was not the kind of otherness and strangeness
> that we had foreseen and expected,
> and he thus remained in fact unrecognized.
> But should not that in itself prove him to be
> the *really* quite other,
> he who casts overboard our notions of otherness
> and thereby shows himself to be
> the one and only genuinely quite other?[14]

So his death is not peripheralized or explained away but it becomes part of the core of the good news.

The death is to be remembered. It played a crucial role in the salvation of the people. It is not an accidental item that, with a bit of luck, could have gone some other way. The death of Jesus is God himself at his saving work. Jesus' death "for us" separates those who understand the meaning of his life from those who wanted to see in him a political deliverer. His victory is over sin and guilt and death, and his triumph is visible only in the after-death world. That message appeals to those who see themselves in the grip of sin and guilt and death.

The supper-ritual keeps the shameful death of Jesus in the forefront of the preaching with remorseless persistence. At the heart of the preaching of the earliest Christians stands a horror that they are revealing to Israel—an unimaginable horror: the Messiah has come and been shamefully dealt with, even to a criminal's death! The Messiah's coming has revealed the murderous heart of this generation. All have played a part in his death.

Just as each one of the earliest disciples had gone through the experience of watching Jesus die, and felt the painful knowledge of themselves that came out of it, so, too, the new converts are invited to sink down into the truth about themselves, for only that truth will reveal to them the glory of God at work in Jesus.

Joining the community, drawn by the joy, the convert is not allowed to focus only on the resurrection, and the approach of glory. The message is not about a deliverance from having to be honest. This summons to honesty, the essence of the prophetic call, appeals powerfully to those who are open to it. This is the "speaking with authority" that echoes in the heart of the hearer who is prepared.

What if a non-believer were to enter the supper liturgy? He will be attracted by their ruthless honesty about their own sinfulness. He will sense, in their honesty, the power of God at work among the group. "God is truly among you" (1 Corinthians 14:25).

The constant impulse to disappear into a pure, unmixed resurrection-joy is always being corrected by the supper-rituals with their focus on Jesus' death. To meet him as Lord and Christ, the converts must first be willing to encounter their own true selves. Jesus does not save us from having to be honest.

11

The Giant Step

Much has been done swiftly. The preaching has been sharpened and the message is being understood by Hebraists and Hellenists alike. The descriptive titles that have been crafted for Jesus in the exegetical workshop are proving most effective.

Who is Jesus? He is the Messiah and more. What is that "more"? It's what is suggested about Jesus in the "Son of Man" image. He is a character from a heavenly story. His death on earth is actually his triumph in the heavens. That "more" is what is suggested, at first very feebly, in the titles "Son of God" and "Lord."

Perhaps asking a slightly different question will help: "Where is Jesus?" He is no longer just an earthly event, or a merely human person. He has been lifted above human history. He hovers somewhere between the world and God. There is a space up there and that is where Jesus is.

This may seem to be a good opportunity for the early disciples to slow things down. Everything has been developing rapidly. Now is the moment for them to pause and to take a look at where the community is and where it is going. But they cannot control it. The context they are in is a peculiar one. In elevating Jesus to a lofty position, they are not raising him to a level that is uninhabited. The space between God and the world is chock-full of personages, powers, spirits, and divine viceroys. Both the Jews and the Gentiles are familiar with more-than-human forms who share in some way God's power over human lives.

This peculiarity of the age in which they live will leave no time for a coffee break in the exegetical workshop. They have raised Jesus to a level where he begins at once to bump into other similarly lofty figures. The community is forced to start spelling out the relationship between them and Jesus. This will lead to much greater clarity on the identity of Jesus himself.

One instance of a more than human figure in the Jewish world of Jesus' day is Wisdom. Wisdom is God's wisdom, but Wisdom is also spoken of as a person in her own right—for Wisdom is portrayed as a woman.

> What Wisdom is and how she came to be
> I shall proclaim;
> and I shall conceal no secrets from you,...
> She is a breath of the might of God,
> and a pure emanation of the glory of the Almighty;...
> For she is a reflection of the eternal light,
> spotless mirror of the power of God,
> the image of his goodness.
> — Wisdom 6:22; 7:25-26

She is imagined as an intimate of God:

> She adds to nobility the splendor of companionship with God;
> Even the Ruler of all loved her.
> For she leads into the understanding of God,
> and chooses his works.
> — Wisdom 8:3-4

She is portrayed as God's vicegerent:

> [Wisdom] preserved the first-formed father of the world
> when he alone had been created;
> And she raised him up from his fall,
> and gave him power to rule all things.
> When... the earth was flooded,
> Wisdom again saved it.
> — Wisdom 10:1-2, 4

The Apostle Philip is part of a Hellenist group that each evening scours the Scriptures for help in their Temple preaching. The

Book of Wisdom proves to be a goldmine. Reading it now, its pertinence fills him with excitement. But it poses a question: What is the relationship between Wisdom, this wonderwoman, and Jesus? They are both inhabiting the same space! At first the question is just a distraction as he reads, but very soon it rises into full consciousness. Philip shares it with Stephen and the other readers.

It is not clear how to conceive of Wisdom—is it other than God, or is it just an attribute of God that is being spoken of as a person but only metaphorically?

> 'To you, O people, I call;
> my appeal is to you mortals.
> You naïve ones, gain prudence,
> you fools, gain sense.
> For noble things I speak;...'
> — Proverbs 8:4-6

Philip can imagine Jesus' voice speaking these same words! Is Jesus' message the same as that of Wisdom, or is it quite different? As they study the texts, they become aware: "We have a problem."

In Genesis 5:18, a disciple reads of the birth of another more-than-human figure, Enoch, the son of Jared. After the return of the Jewish People from the exile in Babylon, Enoch played a major role in the new literature. In Genesis 5:22, we have the sentence: "Enoch walked with God." As time passed this led to raising Enoch to a level of great importance. He began to be seen as one who would play a major role at the end-time. He was given the title, "son of man," which included his being the central figure in fulfilling the hopes of Israel for redemption. Enoch was to triumph over the wicked and save the just.

How does the new role of Jesus relate to Enoch's role in the end-time? Is he Enoch? Hardly. Has Enoch then been replaced, or are they going to work together?

Here is another text from Scripture that had sparked a long development:

> 'See, I am sending an angel before you,
> to guard you on the way....

Do not rebel against him, for he will not forgive your sin,
for my name is in him.
— Exodus 23:20, 21

In Jewish literature angels had figured frequently, and some of them are filled with splendor and power and are described with the same images that are used to describe God! This practice is present also at the monastery of Qumran. There, the final salvation of the chosen will come about through the destruction of evil by the power of "the princely Angel of the kingdom of Michael." It is a widespread notion in Israel at this time.

Up in that superhuman world, the space between God and the human, there exist these great figures, agents of the divine will. How does Jesus relate to them? They are also seen as saviors. How does his role relate to theirs?

But the pressure to speculate about Jesus' identity does not come originally from the Jewish religious world. In the Greek-speaking synagogue with its Hellenist culture the reflection on Jesus is to develop quickly. Theirs is a culture filled with fear and uncertainty, for the Hellenistic heavens are not the abode of angels of salvation and redeemer figures.

The Greek scientists had driven the old gods from Mount Olympus. Zeus and Apollo had never been seen as quite so involved and supportive of human life as the God of Israel. But they could, at least, be engaged in dialogue. Now they are gone. Where do the new gods live? Where do you now go to dialogue with the powerful forces that govern human life?

Most people believe that the new powers dwell in the stars and the planets. The imperturbable march of the stars, inevitably moving in their predictable paths from night to night and season to season—that is the iron face of the forces that rule human life.

The temple where you once prayed to Zeus is replaced by the astrologer who can read the stars, and tell you whether the unchangeable laws are in a favorable sequence or not. If the signs are favorable, you act; if they are unfavorable, you stay indoors. A fatalism takes over when Zeus and his family depart. The new powers are quite indifferent to human beings. Just as you cannot hope to change the path of the stars and the planets, no more can you change what is going to happen to you. It has all been set in motion from the moment of your birth. The line-up of the stars and the planets and the moon at the moment of your birth is your fate: what stars were you born under?

Above the human world are the heavenly spheres, circling one outside the other, each following its own laws. Everything beneath them is in their control. Freedom is a dream about escaping through the spheres, and breaking into the last circle, the Empyrean. There were cults that arose, competitors of the astrologers, that offered a way out to the believer.

You can pray to Serapis:

'Preserve me from the might of the stars,
Hold me back from the cruel compulsion of fate,
Allot me a happy destiny,
Bless my life, O Lord, with all goodness.'

You can pray a Hermetic prayer to be free to live your own life:

'No threatening shall obtain power over me.
No spirit, no demon, no ghost,
nor any other evil apparition
from the underworld shall oppose me,
because of thy name which I bear in my heart.'[15]

How does Jesus relate to the star-gods, the preternatural forces that live in the upper spheres, and govern human life with desolating results, and unbreakable inevitability? This pessimistic mindset is a poison infecting Hellenistic culture. There is a bondage and a groaning and a yearning to be free.

It is difficult for us to imagine such a widespread cultural slave-mentality. Perhaps an experience I had as a teacher might help.

It was the first day of class, a religion class. Before the students could know me and where I was coming from, I gave a quiz, a single question: "If you were to learn with certainty that there is no God, how would you feel?" Almost half the students, seniors in a Catholic high school, expressed relief at the thought. If there is no God, they can be free to relax, they can lead their own lives. Their

God was a hostile presence, and freedom was to be out from under his power.

That is the world of the Hellenists.

Even in the Hellenist synagogues, that cultural reality has force. It is part of what you pick up as you learn Greek, just as in our day, you learn our science as you learn our language. As a result there is a problem in the Hellenists' synagogue that is not that noticeable among the Hebraists. The upcountry apostles are far less caught up in the world of astral powers, archons, spheres, and the iron laws of Necessity. While the Hellenists can translate the Aramaic hymns and faith-formulas into Greek, and understand them and enjoy them, for they live in both worlds, the Aramaic synagogue lives within the Scriptures.

But among the Greek-speakers a certain inadequacy is found in the hymns and the formulas. Stephen and the more cosmopolitan disciples among the Hellenists feel that the spectacular nature of the Good News is not yet shining forth clearly in the hymns and formulas. They can understand why—it is the difference in cultures.

Their day-to-day scene is part of the Empire-wide world where devout Jews live side by side with pagans. Their pagan neighbors' thinking is riddled with fear and uncertainty.

Stephen and his community are familiar with this world. The cultured men and women of the Empire, the "moderns," take this fatal necessity for granted. It is the backdrop of their lives. It is so widely accepted that inquiring too closely into a person's time of birth is known to be a hostile act. It is a way of finding out a time when they can be attacked successfully, a day of vulnerability. Those who were caught searching into an emperor's astrological forecast were treated as traitors. Anyone who got into magic was a source of fear to others. Perhaps, by chance, he would discover some incantation that would give him control of these astral energies.

Stephen knows that the fear of superhuman powers is a constant factor in people's lives, a nightmare that haunts them. Even for some of the earliest converts, this is a major question. "The Jesus-Event is wonderful, and that he has been enthroned is splendid, but… what about the powers of the Cosmos? Are the superhuman forces that live in the heavens and must be propitiated—are they now not to be feared? What about this incident, or that one, where their strength and hostility were clearly on display?"

It comes up constantly, and Stephen is forced to spell out the Good News constantly: Jesus is now enthroned above all the cosmic powers. They have been rendered powerless. How can that be? Why does the return to life of a Messiah for the Jews make any difference in the power structure of the heavens? So Stephen has to make it very explicit. "This is what the Jesus-Event really means! It is an ultimate good news, and there is no power left to deal with except Jesus. He is seated above all the cosmic powers. He has become the source of a victorious final confidence. The last battle has been won!"

There is no arguing, no effort to prove. As Jesus simply asserted the truth, so too does Stephen. The truth will find its own hearers. The conviction that Jesus is the centerpiece of human history and of each individual's life, and that there is no perceptible limit to the meaningfulness of the Jesus-Event, is the foundation of all the early hymns.

It leads to a dramatic discovery. Here are the steps that are taken: whatever is the complete meaning of human life must have been present at the beginning of human life. If Jesus is the full, final meaning of human history, how could he have been an afterthought? He is now God's final plenipotentiary. Does not that marvelous finale throw light on the whole course of human history—even back to the very beginning? Can he possibly be the fullness of the process *now* if he had been absent at the beginning of it all?

Certainly he was present at the creation in the mind of God. But is that enough? Is it possible that he was present when the spheres were set in motion and when the unchangeable laws were laid down? When he was enthroned at the resurrection, was he entering the heavens for the first time, or was he returning home?

> From the womb, before the dawn, I begot you.
> — Psalm 110:3

They have already applied this text to Jesus. It strongly suggests that the Messiah, the Christ, had been God's Son from the beginning. But that suggestion is not focused on at first. "When did Jesus become the Son of God?" That question has to be asked before the phrase, "before the dawn," can be appreciated. That question arises when the Hellenist leaders are faced with the question of relating Jesus to the powers and energies present in the heavens.

> The Lord begot me, the beginning of his works,
> The forerunner of his deeds of long ago;
> From of old, I was formed,
> at the first, before the earth.
> — Proverbs 8:22-23

This text from Proverbs has been applied to Jesus in an earlier effort to spell out the full meaning of the resurrection. Now it takes on a new perspective. A new question has arisen: when did Jesus become God's Son?

> When there were no deeps, I was brought forth,
> when there were no fountains or springs of water;
> Before the mountains were settled into place,
> before the hills, I was brought forth.
> — Proverbs 8:24-25

What is it like for Stephen and the leaders of the Hellenists to hear this text read out one day when their minds are filled with the question about how this Jesus, the risen Messiah of Israel, is related to the cosmic powers who had taken the place of the old gods driven from Olympus by Greek science?

> When the earth and fields were not yet made,
> or the first clods of the world,
> when he established the heavens, there was I... ,
> Then was I beside him, as artisan,
> I was his delight day by day,
> playing before him all the while,
> playing over the whole of his earth.
> — Proverbs 8:26-27, 30-31

It is this community, formed for those who do not know Aramaic, that takes the next step, a giant step. It is filled with dangers that are not obvious at first.

The two different ways that the two cultures had of filling up the space between the world and God have a role in this development. The Wisdom figure of the Jewish tradition and the astral forces of the Hellenistic heavens go to work together in the consciousness of the Hellenist Christians. Jesus must have been in existence even before the world. It is the only answer that makes sense of their experience of his power. There is no debate; it is clear the minute the question arises.

> But you (Bethlehem) Ephrathah,
> least among the clans of Judah,
> from you shall come forth for me one who is to be ruler in Israel;
> whose origin is from of old,
> from ancient times.
> He shall take his place as shepherd
> by the strength of the LORD,
> by the majestic name of the LORD, his God;
> and they shall dwell securely, for now his greatness shall reach to the ends of the earth.
> — Micah 5:1, 3

However Wisdom had been pictured up to now—as an entity other than God or a personified divine attribute—*now* Wisdom is a person!

Is Jesus being seen as divine? That is not the question. He is Wisdom and that means he pre-existed the world. Was he uncreated? That also is not the question, and as long as there is no question, there is no response. In some of the texts Wisdom is seen as created, in others as begotten.

Doesn't the title, Son of God, spell out his divinity? No. It leaves the question open. What *is* being said? Jesus who is the complete and final meaning of human history was the meaning of history right from the start. All of history has always been inside of *his* reality.

Had he created the world? That had been suggested of Wisdom. God had first produced Wisdom, and Wisdom had created the world. So that suggestion does enter the earliest formulas of faith.

> There is one God,
> the Father, from whom all things are
> and for whom we exist,
> and one Lord, Jesus Christ,
> through whom all things are
> and through whom we exist.
> — 1 Corinthians 8:6

He was pre-existent. He had been there before the world. He had been present at the creation. He who is the centerpiece of it all, the one to whom all power at the end-time has been given, had already been filled with power at the beginning.

This means that Jesus had been "sent" into the world, and it fits their memories of the way Jesus had spoken of himself. He had seen his life as a being-sent. He had imagined himself as a missionary. He had formed a group to continue that mission.

> When the fullness of time had come,
> God sent his Son, born of a woman,
> born under the law,
> to ransom those under the law.
> — Galatians 4:4

So, he had been sent. It is the obvious conclusion from his pre-existence. He had been in the heavenly sphere, and he had descended. He had come down through the spheres and he had become incarnate. He had humbled himself. His willingness to be crucified was only the last step in a humiliation he had chosen in his pre-existent state when he had decided to descend through the spheres.

This is the real dignity of the one whom they had betrayed, and denied, and abandoned.

Before moving to the more explicit statements of the pre-existence of Jesus, there is a strange and intricate example that can help get at the way the minds of the Hellenists were working at this moment in the earliest Church. This text is read aloud at a synagogue service:

> The LORD spoke to Moses and said, 'Take the staff and assemble the community, you and Aaron, your brother, and in their presence command the rock to yield its waters. Thereby you will bring forth water from the rock for them, and supply the community and their livestock with water.'
> — Numbers 20:7-8

Those among the disciples who had been trained in the Torah and the Prophets are familiar with a rabbinic teaching that this rock actually followed the people of Israel during their stay in the desert, providing them with water. The water-giving rock had moved about, keeping close to the camp.

There is also a text in Wisdom that commented on the desert wandering, and how the chosen people had been cared for.

> The holy people and their blameless descendants—
> it was she who rescued them from the nation that oppressed them....
> She gave the holy ones the rewards of their labors;
> Conducted them by a wondrous road,
> became a shelter for them by day
> a starry flame by night....
> water was given them from the sheer rock,
> a quenching of their thirst from the hard stone.
> — Wisdom 10:15, 17; 11:4

Hovering over the whole desert experience was the instrument of God's providential care, Wisdom, just as she had been present at the creation. To Wisdom is attributed what Exodus had said of God. As one of the disciples hears this text, he wonders: if Wisdom was present in the desert, what of Jesus? Where had he been?

He answers it this way:

> All ate the same spiritual food,
> and all drank the same spiritual drink,

for they drank from a spiritual rock that followed them,
and the rock was the Christ.
— 1 Corinthians 10:4

The visible Jesus who had lived such a short life, had been living another life. His earthly existence was just a part of his story. To understand him and the meaning of his days on earth, you have to see his full story. The Apostles are those who had been with him "from the beginning." By that "beginning" they meant the day Jesus went to the Jordan, to John, to be baptized by him. Now the Hellenists grasp that even that is not enough to understand him. He is not merely of this world. He had pre-existed it. In his pre-existent state, he had deliberately chosen to involve himself in human history. He received a mission to save the people. He was there in the desert with the chosen people. Only at the very end has his mission become visible and, even then, for just a brief time.

Their conviction that Jesus is pre-existent still leaves many questions unanswered, because these questions had not yet been asked. Still it is an immense step, and a step that is to have unexpected consequences for the little communities.

12

The Great Hymns

The proclamation of the pre-existence of Jesus was an immense step for the early Church. For the disciples to see Jesus as Messiah is to see him very much as a part of the human story. "Son of David" ties him to the human race. He has his origins here where we can see him.

"Son of God" lifts him off the ground like an immense brightly-colored balloon. There's a definite straining at the ropes that keep him attached to earth. But the title is so ambiguous it doesn't snap the cables.

But pre-existence is the tearing loose from the merely human. Jesus is being seen as a superhuman reality involved in a cosmic drama—in fact, he is playing the lead role. There was much in Jesus' words that fitted this suprahistorical personage. Much that the disciples had ignored now came back to them, and helped them realize that Jesus had known all along what now they were glimpsing. He had talked of "being-sent," but they had heard that as a synonym for being called to prophesy. In the greater story that was occurring in the heavens, the very act that here on earth symbolized absolute defeat—death—was the moment when victory was won.

His words at the supper had been so assured. They had felt it and attributed it at the time to his anticipation of a triumphal, imminent intervention of God. His suggestions that he was about to die did not register. But now it comes to them: they had barely known him. He had been alone in his awareness of the cosmic struggle that he was engaged in.

Now as they come to recognize the deeper level of his reality, they find him waiting there, welcoming them. He had known all along that they would come to this. His words at that last meal, "You still do not know me," take on a new meaning. Most of what he was has been hidden from them.

This is what pre-existence involves. He is afloat above human history. It reveals their failure to believe. His ordinary appearance to their eyes had made them deaf to what he was saying so clearly.

How can anyone come to believe that a very human acquaintance of theirs began life before the foundation of the world, someone who had to eat or go hungry, to sleep or become tired? Why, he had a moment when he was born and a moment when he died just like everyone else! We can imagine the heroes of the distant past this way, but to reach such a conviction about a table companion demands an event of unprecedented impact. Such was Jesus' life and death, and his extraordinary appearances after death, the Jesus-Event.

At their supper-ritual the cosmic background of the Messiah Jesus strains to be expressed. In the Temple and the synagogue, the forms are fixed. But the supper-ritual is open, and the early efforts to use the psalms prove inadequate. No psalm says it quite right. Their phrases are indirect and clumsy. As the convictions of the disciples clarify they demand clearer expression.

Pre-existence is no sooner realized than it is embodied in a hymn by the charismatic leader of the Hellenist synagogue, Stephen. It is the most famous of the early hymns.

> Though Jesus was in the form of God.
> he did not regard equality with God
> something to be grasped.
> Jesus emptied himself,
> taking the form of a slave,
> coming in human likeness,
> and found human in appearance…
> For this, God greatly exalted him
> and bestowed on him the Name
> that is above every name,
> that at the name of Jesus
> every knee should bend,
> in the heavens, on earth, and under the earth.

and every tongue confess
that Jesus, the Messiah, is Lord.
— Philippians 2:6-11

It is learned with great enthusiasm, and the Hellenists are a very demanding audience. When they found "son of man" not useful in expressing their sense of Jesus, they soon dropped it. But this new song strikes a solid note. It says better than anything that has preceded it what the Hellenists have been feeling but had not found a way to express.

With this hymn, the Jesus-Event is launched into the world of Greek culture. It is like the discovery of the Pacific Ocean. In the new language, Jesus is somewhat unrecognizable, and yet it is devout Jews who have made the transition, not converts from paganism. In order to satisfy the needs of the diaspora experience of the Jewish people, the meaning of Jesus' death and resurrection has to be translated into a culture that is far removed from the ways of thinking with which the Hebraist congregation is comfortable. Fortunately this early effort is a splendid one.

The focus of the hymn is the enthronement of Jesus, and his entry into God's power. Jesus has become God's viceroy. The high point of the hymn is the cry "Jesus is Lord," the acclamation used by the disciples since the earliest supper-rituals. This gives the hymn a very familiar note. It is nothing but another way of saying what they have been saying at the suppers all along.

The familiar cry is raised aloft again, but now there are new voices shouting it besides the earliest Christians. Besides the tongues of the disciples, there are voices *under* the earth and in the heavens that have joined in. It is no longer just a room filled with earthling worshippers. The veil hiding the heavens from view is now drawn back, and all through the heavenly spheres, and in the worlds beneath the earth, the same cry of praise to Jesus is raised, his power is acknowledged.

God enthrones Jesus at his right hand before an audience which contains all those who reside in the space above the world, all of the cosmic powers. Jesus is more than human: how does he relate to the other more than human forces that govern human life? He is their new Lord. Human life is freed as it passes under the control of Jesus. He is the only power to be reckoned with.

How did this enthronement come about? "Through his death" is the familiar answer. Now the composer adds a quite new suggestion: "and through his willingness to be born." Jesus is not called from tending his sheep, or from working his plough. He is called from his place in the heavens where he exists in the form of God, and he is sent into the world.

Long before the surrender of Jesus in the garden, accepting his death, there had been another decision that he made that was vital for human salvation. Indeed, these two decisions are but one. They are the beginning and the end of a decision originally taken in the heavens by one who dwelt there with God. It was a decision to set aside a great dignity and to accept humiliation. Because of that decision, God has exalted Jesus to his right hand.

The dignity suggested for the pre-existent Messiah is not the central theme of the hymn. It is brought in to illustrate the cosmic importance of Jesus' willingness to die. His death is the be-all and the end-all of human history. The Lordship of the heavenly spheres is involved. This hymn is a way of explaining the universal importance of the death of Jesus and his resurrection.

The hymn gets an enthusiastic reaction in the Hellenist community. The author has echoed the community's experience. It is soon translated into Aramaic, and used at a supper-ritual with the Apostles present.

How do they react? Did they murmur, or shift in their seats uncomfortably? Do they feel that the Jesus they had known is being twisted into an unrecognizable shape by the new hymn? Do they experience a sense of wariness that Jesus is being used for purposes that were never his? Not at all! The disagreements in the early Church are not about Jesus. The two communities are in step on the pre-existence. The new hymn fits the convictions of the Apostles like a glove.

The disciples find in it a wonderful expression of their deepest convictions. There is no sense that something new is being squeezed in, and that the Jesus they knew so well is being made over. No, this is the Jesus they had come to know in his life, death, and rising. This is exactly what his resurrection means. How else can you express the fact that history comes to a single point in Jesus?

Some elements of the early Church seem so fortuitous. Because

Jesus abruptly makes a ritual of his death, early Christians end up with a gathering that is largely unprogrammed. That empty field gives play to the creation and singing of original hymns.

Because there are diaspora Jews, the early Church quickly becomes two separate synagogues. But they keep very close links. There are some disciples who are at home in both languages and both cultures. Each of the communities is very aware of what is happening in the other. In that sense, there is but one mind and one heart. They experience themselves as one body of disciples.

But the differences are there, and they prove important in the way the Church grows.

One of the Apostles had composed a hymn for the Hebraist synagogue just as Stephen had for the Greek-speakers. It is later quoted by Paul in his First Letter to the Corinthians.

> Jesus died for our sins
> in accordance with the Scriptures;
> he was buried;
> he was raised on the third day
> in accordance with the Scriptures;
> he appeared to Cephas,
> then to the twelve.
> — 1 Corinthians 15:3-5

The contrast between these two hymns reveals the different cultural worlds of the two early communities.

This is the world of the Apostles. The Jewish inheritance of the early disciples dominates the text. The prophets are the ones who explain the meaning of Jesus. Scripture is used to explain the facts of his death and resurrection. Sin and forgiveness must be preached.

Notice how different this is from the hymn Paul quotes in his letter to the Philippians. In this hymn the focus is on the human life of Jesus: there is no mention of the pre-existent "form of God" who descends into the human sphere. For the Hebraists the old and the new covenant as they are described in the Scriptures explain Jesus' role as Messiah. The Hellenic context of two worlds, the heavens and the earth, and the One who passes from one to the other isn't here. In place of the obedience of the pre-existent "form of God," here we have his death for the sins of his people. In the Apostolic synagogue we have an audience that turns to Scripture to solve its problems. Among the Greek speakers, the descent and the obedience of the pre-existent One is of meaning to everyone on earth who lives under the governance of the heavenly powers.

For the Aramaic group, the resurrection is explicit and central. It is the necessary answer to the problem of a Messiah who has been put to death. Only his resurrection can raise this man to the Messianic level, and in their hymn the risen Lord appears to his disciples.

But with the Hellenists, the focus is different: the enthroned Lord receives the homage of the angels and the supra-human powers. In Stephen's hymn, the resurrection and the appearances to the disciples are skipped over. Jesus goes from his humiliation to his enthronement.

In the one we have people who need to hear the words of forgiveness from the lips of Jesus, their Lord. This is the milieu of the Apostolic band. In the other, Jesus is shown to be in complete control of human destiny, the newly enthroned Lord of the heavens and the earth, the only one who can deliver those enslaved by hostile cosmic powers.

These two small communities are side by side in Jerusalem, separated by language but experiencing a common conviction about the unlimited significance of Jesus. One group expresses this in a way that makes Jesus shine forth to those whose world is the world of Scripture. The other group seeks for ways to make Jesus' significance intelligible to the Hellenic world that they live in.

These are not sharp distinctions. Judaism had itself been touched by Hellenic culture over the centuries, and the Greek-speaking Jews of Jerusalem are trained in the Scriptures, too. The borderline between the two congregations is a fuzzy one, and some individuals cross it regularly.

But there is a difference. The Hellenists are very conscious of the larger world of the Empire. In their desire to express the limitless meaning they find in Jesus, they must relate him to the cosmic forces that govern human life. This propels them along a path that finds his pre-existence essential, as well as his part in the creation of the world. He must be recognized as having been there from the beginning. He had encompassed the human story at both ends and, by actually entering it, he had given it a heavenly form that can absorb the believers and bring them to the glory of the risen state.

13

The Logical Conclusions

Each day the disciples go up to the Temple as they had done whenever Jesus had been with them in Jerusalem. Nothing that comes out of the exegetical workshop makes the disciples feel uncomfortable at the Temple sacrifices.

That Jesus is alive and active, that he is Lord of the heavens and the earth and the underworld, that he had been present at the creation of the world—none of this new awareness disturbs their devotion when they join in the Temple services. They find being present at worship there thoroughly meaningful even though Jesus' name is never once mentioned. That lack appears to them as a problem that they themselves will rectify.

By their preaching they hope to convert Israel to an acknowledgment that Jesus is now the viceroy of God. The defect of omitting Jesus' name in the services is for now made up for by his being named constantly in their preaching. For the disciples it is still all of a piece, Temple and table.

Linking Jesus and Wisdom does not undo their sense of being fully Jewish. That Jesus is now known to have pre-existed the world does not immediately result in questioning the value of the Temple. Wisdom does not have the solidity of independent existence that the cosmic powers of the Hellenistic world do. So the image of Jesus can easily take on the role of Wisdom.

Among the Greek-speakers it is not the same. The cosmic powers that rule from the heavens are dethroned at Jesus' entry into the heavenly realms.

But there is in Judaism, too, a real figure who looms large, too large to be ignored, and too real to be absorbed by Jesus, and that is

Moses. What is the relationship between Jesus and Moses? Moses is the source of God's Law and of the ritual worship of the Temple, and Jesus is the viceroy of God.

What is it like for an early Christian to hear read in the synagogue these words:

> Since then no prophet has arisen in Israel like Moses,
> whom the LORD knew face to face.
> – Deuteronomy 34:10

One day at the synagogue service, one of the Apostles reads aloud the text:

> From Jacob came the man
> who would win the favor of all the living.
> Dear to God and human beings,
> Moses, whose memory is a blessing.
> God made him like the angels in honor.
> – Sirach 45:1-2

Many traditions had developed over the centuries about Moses. They reached the point where in Philo's writings, Moses is made a partner of God, and is given "the whole world as a possession suitable for his heir."[16]

On Sinai, Moses "was said to have entered into the darkness where God was, that is, into the invisible, and shapeless, and incorporeal world, the essence, which is the model of all existing things," there beholding "things invisible to mortal nature."[17]

What is his relation to Jesus? This question is to become a vital concern, first of all in the Hellenist synagogue. Moses means nothing to the Roman world that will be their audience. Can Jesus be explained to that world without Moses being mentioned?

Especially pressing is a question that concerns Moses' authority as the one who reveals God's will.

> Because of his trustworthiness and meekness
> God selected him from all flesh;
> He let him hear his voice,

and led him into the cloud,
where he handed over the commandments,
the law of life and understanding,
that he might teach his precepts to Jacob,
his judgments and decrees to Israel.
— Sirach 45:4-6

Moses is the one who has revealed the mind of God. He spelled out the path that must be followed if life and knowledge are to be theirs. That path has become the way of life of the chosen people, and it is at the heart of their day-to-day world. It governs their choices. It plays a big part in the disciples' schedule.

How does the path Jesus has given to them relate to the path handed down to them from Moses? What about the Torah? Does it have any further use? What of the Temple and the sacrifices? Are they still relevant in the end-time? Is it possible that with the risen Jesus all has been changed?

It is in the Hellenist gathering that people begin to struggle with this question. Stephen is especially bothered by the problem. He does not like the prospect of having to introduce his pagan neighbors to the traditions of Moses. It is unnecessary baggage and it will keep them from hearing the gospel.

One afternoon Stephen hears Philip telling a few of the newly converted about the day Jesus dramatically cleared the Temple of the moneychangers. Stephen has heard it before but now he hears it afresh, and two texts he had memorized years before come to mind. Here is the first text:

All who keep the Sabbath without profaning it
and hold fast to my covenant,
them I will bring to my holy mountain
and make them joyful in my house of prayer.
Their burnt offerings and their sacrifices
will be acceptable on my altar,
for my house shall be called
a house of prayer for *all* peoples.
— Isaiah 56:6-7

The prophet is declaring the lofty role of the Temple and its rituals, and attributing this practice to God's will. God is behind the Temple practices. Even the great prophet Isaiah is endorsing Moses as the one who truly heard God, and revealed His will to Israel. Is this still the case, even now in the end-time? Is that what God wants?

He then recalls a second text that centers around the Temple—this one from another prophet:

> Do you think you can steal and murder, commit adultery and perjury, sacrifice to Baal, follow other gods that you do not know, and then come and stand in my presence in this house, which bears my name, and say, 'We are safe! We can commit all these abominations again!'? Has this house which bears my name become in your eyes a den of thieves?
> — Jeremiah 7:9-11

Has not what God willed to be a house of prayer been turned into a den of thieves by the chosen people! Isn't this a sign that the Temple's role is over?

But Jesus himself had attended the Temple and was filled with devotion for it. Stephen's reasoning winds itself into a tight knot. But nothing is yet clear.

As the days pass, the fermenting goes on, accompanied by discovering other texts that seem relevant, and recalling other remarks of Jesus. Certain texts that they memorized long before begin to cluster around the question, along with incidents from Jesus' life. It is still not a central issue, but it is on the move and gathering steam.

Questions are being asked at the same time that all are going daily to the Temple. It is still just a wondering.

Stephen finally cuts the knot when he hears this text from the Book of Deuteronomy:

> Since then no prophet has arisen in Israel like Moses, whom the LORD knew face to face.
> — Deuteronomy 34:10

Can it be that Jesus is just one episode in salvation history? Can there be elements like the Temple and the Torah that stand on a par with him?

Stephen challenges it with words of Jesus he had been told about:

> The law and the prophets lasted until John,
> but from then on the kingdom of God is proclaimed.
> — Luke 16:16

There are many such indications in Jesus' preaching that see the Law as of a limited nature. In fact, isn't there a tension between Law and prophecy already present in the Scriptures? Prophecy points to a future when Law will be surpassed by a history-shaking event. Believing in Jesus and his resurrection is a choice of prophecy over Law. Jesus is the fulfillment of Scripture itself because he is fulfilling all the prophecies—that is the central thrust of the earliest Temple preaching. The disciples use the sacred text as a source of promises, promises whose fulfillment is the abrogation of Torah!

That's what comes into view first: that the Jesus-Event has become the total meaning of human life. Even the Law of Moses can have meaning only within the Jesus-Event. Since Jesus is the totality of God's actions toward humans, then it must hold true for everyone, Jew and Greek.

The Apostles had returned to Jerusalem because they felt themselves sent by Jesus to give Israel a last chance before the final curtain fell. But Stephen is now offering a corrective. Jesus had died for *all*. The good news must be preached to all.

Just as he is himself experiencing a rich meaningfulness in his own life, Stephen knows that those living far from Jerusalem are to be included in Jesus' mission. Stephen knows that the concern he feels for all of them must be from Jesus. Just as Jesus was sent and died for all, so the disciples must preach the word to all. Everyone who groans under the blind rule of the cosmic powers has to hear about Jesus.

Jesus is the new ground of salvation: whatever value is left in Moses is within the salvation brought by Jesus.

> Everyone who calls upon the name of the Lord will be saved.
> —Joel 3:5

That is the path to salvation, Jesus the Lord, not the Law. Jesus is above the Law which had handed him over to be cursed.

> If a man guilty of a capital offense is put to death,
> and you hang him on a tree,
> his corpse shall not remain on the tree overnight.
> You must bury it the same day;
> anyone who is hanged is a curse of God.
> —Deuteronomy 21:22-23

Their opponents had used this text against the early disciples. As a result, it becomes a source of reflection for them. Though Jesus was condemned by the Law, yet he is the totality of God's will. He stands above the Law. God has a will that is higher than the Mosaic Law.

Why, the Law itself was given through Moses by Wisdom. Just as Wisdom cannot possibly be a reality independent of Jesus, neither can the Law.

But if the Law no longer contains the will of God—for that will had become an invitation to call on the Name—then what of the Temple and the sacrifices?

To answer the objection that their Messiah had died as a criminal, the disciples were forced to enter into the significance of his death. Had Jesus ended his years of preaching with an ascension instead of a crucifixion, the question would not have come up. But this ignominious death has occurred, and their opponents use it to prove that he is not the Messiah. His death, then, becomes a focus of reflection and rapid speculative development. The Deuteronomy texts go from becoming proofs against his claims to an assertion: "Yes, he is not within that Law. He is outside of it, because he is above it. He is a wholly new speaking of God and he reveals God's will to be so different from what had been believed. Instead of telling us his Law, God has, in Jesus, sent us the fulfillment of his will, and our salvation consists in our calling on Jesus' name."

The two threads interweave, Jesus-as-Wisdom and Jesus-versus-the-Law. For the Hellenists, it is the latter that provides the primary impulse: since Jesus is God's final word, he cannot have a peer in Moses whose Law and Temple are so narrow, and so sectarian, so irrelevant to current human problems. Jesus is good news precisely because he reveals a salvation aimed at *everyone*. Everyone needs what he had won through his death. The Good News is for everybody.

Yet these speculations are taking place among people who are devout Jews, people who are going to the Temple and the synagogue regularly, people who cannot imagine breaking with the Law. The disciples are being forced along a path of thinking that is very new to them. They are feeling their way into the deeper dimensions of the Jesus-Event the way a man in a dark and unfamiliar basement feels with his fingers along a wall. They are pushed forward by their need to proclaim that God has, in Jesus, communicated himself in a final form that can never be surpassed. It is not immediately obvious what this involves. It becomes so only step by step.

The boldness of this enterprise is incredible: these are devout Jews, conscious of being "The Chosen," filled with trust in their adherence to Moses, the basis of their sense of salvation up to now, and they are taking steps that will lead to a break with the ritual regulations of the Torah, and with the Temple cult.

Without a powerful conviction that Jesus is clothed with God's authority by his resurrection, this movement would have gone nowhere. Without an assurance that the Jesus they knew meant them to go this way, they would never have gone. They are experiencing an invitation to experiment their way into the mystery. Certain memories of Jesus are used as confirmations of the path they are taking. In their vivid recollections of him they find enough of a basis for their speculating that the Temple has been replaced by a people, living stones, and that the sacrifices have ended with Jesus' death, and that the Law has been transcended by the kingdom, God's gift in Jesus.

14

Antioch and Jerusalem

In Jerusalem Israel speaks two languages, and there is little interaction between the two language groups. What happens in the Aramaic neighborhoods is of little interest to the Greek-speaking neighborhoods, and vice versa. Each language group has its own culture as well.

Each culture has its own concerns. People gossip about the personages and events that count in their parts of town. The two sections are largely self-contained. Most have never walked in the other neighborhoods. Instead of interacting, the two groups run along parallel lines with distinct histories.

Had there been an Aramaic newspaper in Jerusalem, the stories would have made no sense to the Greeks—even if they were translated for them. The people named would be strangers and the disputes unintelligible. That was much more the case with Jerusalem's larger population of Aramaic speakers. What went on in the Greek-speaking neighborhoods was of little interest to them.

The Apostles and their followers were mostly outsiders in Jerusalem. They attended local synagogues where they were not noticed as being at all different from anyone else. When they did mention Jesus to those outside their little family, they presented him as the Messiah, a term familiar to their listeners. But ordinarily they took a back seat at the synagogue services as befitted their status as visitors. They did not try to use the synagogue as a preaching forum. That was left to their work in the Temple.

But for the converted Hellenists Jerusalem is their home. They have been living in neighborhoods where Aramaic is rarely heard. After their baptism in Jesus, the Hellenist disciples continue to attend their neighborhood synagogues. There the services are in Greek. They usually find themselves to be a handful of disciples in the midst of a large assembly.

They are eager to get the word about Jesus out, and at the synagogue service they have their first audiences. They invite people to join them in the new task of the chosen people: to preach to the world the news, "Jesus has unseated the cosmic powers."

Stephen has attended this synagogue since he was a boy, and he knows almost everyone. He is admired, and he easily gains a hearing, and some of his listeners are eager to be baptized.

This is the background for the strangest phrase in the Acts of the Apostles.

> That day saw the beginning of a great persecution of the church in Jerusalem. All except the Apostles scattered throughout the countryside of Judea and Samaria.
> —Acts 8:1

"Except the Apostles." How can that be? How can the Apostles escape a persecution aimed at the followers of Jesus? It happens because the Hellenist converts live in a world quite isolated from the world the Apostles live in. Their need to speak out in their synagogues about Jesus is not felt among the Hebraists.

The Hellenists have audiences that are different from the ones the Apostles are speaking to. The Greek-speaking hearers of the Good News have questions, and they prove very provocative to Stephen and those who are preaching. Speculations on the precise dignity of Jesus quickly become issues.

It forces the leaders of the Hellenist gathering back to the words of Jesus himself, and back to Scripture, in search of answers.

In responding to the new questions the special few who had been with Jesus in his public life recall half-forgotten incidents where Jesus had said something that might be relevant: how Jesus had not been enthusiastic about some of the good and devout people of his world, the Pharisees; how he had preached the kingdom even to religious outcasts; how he had placed all the weight of the Law on the command to love, the need for a new heart present within the worshipper; how he had warned that mere external behavior was not just useless but very dangerous; how he had surrounded himself with a traveling band of men and women, how he had sent them out to preach the kingdom.

Inevitably someone recalled these words of his:

> Eat what is set before you.
> —Luke 10: 8

What was Jesus saying about the traditions of eating? Where do the many regulations concerning food now stand? Can they be ignored now that the end-time is coming?

While these questions begin to crop up, the regular schedule is quite unchanged. The believers are present at the Temple, and take part in the sacrifices, both the Greek speakers and the Aramaic speakers. The slaying and burning involved in the holocausts are still a part of their routine. Their synagogue practices are quite the same as before. When they preach in the Temple, they try very hard to help people see that Jesus is a perfect fit with all that Judaism reverences.

At times, though, questions arise.

Jesus had opened the kingdom to the penitent heart. What of the path through Temple and Torah that had been handed to Israel by God from Moses? Can these two approaches stand side by side?

It is at this point that the different worlds of the two sub-groups within the community of the disciples cause two different histories to come about.

The Greek-speaking disciples, the Hellenists, begin to suggest in their speeches in the Greek-speaking synagogues that the Temple and the Torah have lost their central role. When they speak along this line in the Greek-speaking synagogues, some of the non-Christian hearers are very disturbed. They know that the pagans speak like that, but now to hear it preached by Jews in the synagogues!

Greek-speaking Jews have their own reasons to be attracted by Jesus' teaching. They can see in the new preaching an element of universal-salvation that is most appealing. They cannot easily live with a God who has no concern for the mass of mankind. They have come to know the unbelievers too well and they are filled with a desire to share their Good News with them. Jesus' stress on the heart over the rituals made his message available to everyone. Whenever they get the chance, the disciples in the Greek synagogues speak about Jesus as the fulfillment of the Law and the Prophets.

Now any suggestion that the Law is being surpassed is going to arouse a reaction, especially from those with a Pharisaic background, like Saul of Tarsus. He had been brought to Jerusalem as a child and had been educated by the Pharisees. To such people the preaching of Stephen and the other Hellenist leaders becomes a source of tension.

Though Saul of Tarsus has lived most of his life in Jerusalem, the Apostles do not know him at all.

The devout Jews of the Greek-speaking Jerusalem synagogues who are disturbed by the disciples of Jesus in their midst appeal to their synagogue leaders. A meeting is called to discuss the problems. At this meeting Stephen is given a chance to explain the position of the disciples.

What is it like for these devout Jews to hear his message? A path to salvation is put forward that is strikingly different from the familiar path. Moses, the Temple, and the Torah are being bypassed. It is very confusing. According to the Torah, Jesus' death was a curse, and now these men are saying that Jesus' death is an act of salvation given to all.

Stephen is eloquent and filled with enthusiasm. He has converted many already—or, from the viewpoint of the majority, has led many astray. The scene becomes a wrangle, and a fierce argument breaks out. Many in the group become enraged at what they see as blasphemy, and they take the law into their own hands and stone Stephen to death.

It is a critical moment in the history of the earliest Church. The two branches of the disciples will now be separated by distance as well as by language. They will still keep in touch, but it will not be the very close contact that they have had up to now.

The leaders of the Greek-speaking synagogues in Jerusalem begin a purge, and the followers of Jesus are sought out and expelled. Many of the disciples leave Jerusalem for safer places. Those who were from Galilee head in that direction. They are few—people like Philip and Andrew. On their journey north, they begin to convert some of the Samaritans they meet.

That raises the question: what must be asked of these converts? In addition to accepting Jesus must they conform also to the Jerusalem traditions of Judaism? For the moment it's an occasional thing and there is no time to sort out the answers.

A number of the disciples go to the coastal cities. There they preach in the synagogues and make converts, and small communities are formed. Quite a few go on to Alexandria and even Rome. Some go to Damascus, and many go to the great city of Antioch where there is a large Jewish population and where they have relatives and friends. They preach in the synagogues when the opportunity is given and they begin to convert people to Jesus.

Within two years of Jesus' death, one whole wing of his followers is scattered by this persecution. It appears catastrophic. The sect is barely formed, its leader dead, and now it is forced to flee in many directions. It should spell the end for this sect.

In the thirteenth century, when Saint Dominic began his congregation and it was still a mere handful, he had requests from various dioceses for help. The temptation to stay together until there was a larger manpower pool was great. But he remarked, "Stored in the barn, the grain rots. Scattered to the wind, it bears fruit." To some it appeared a sure path to disintegration, but they were proved wrong. The scattering proved to be a most blessed happening.

This now becomes the history of the Hellenist disciples. As they scatter across the Roman Empire, their message is heard in far distant places, and finds a welcome in the hearts of strangers.

At first these are Jews preaching to Jews. Occasionally a Gentile listens and is converted. In Antioch, within five years of Jesus' death, Gentiles are accepted into the body of the disciples without even being circumcised. This will create tension with the Jerusalem synagogue.

Meanwhile the Apostles and their Aramaic-speaking companions continue to preach in the Temple. They persist in preaching the coming of the end-time, and the need to accept Jesus as the fulfillment of the Law and the Prophets. Without the presence of the more progressive Hellenists, and the constant dialogue that had been influencing both groups, the Jerusalem synagogue becomes somewhat more conservative. It doesn't have to deal with the problems that constantly arose in the Hellenist congregation. A number of Pharisees are converted. Belief in Jesus goes hand in hand with a strict traditional Judaism.

Occasionally people go back and forth between Antioch and Jerusalem. Antioch is a journey of about eight days. The two groups keep in touch, but the daily contact is gone.

It is such an unexpected development. Now the two language groups are separated by distance. Nothing much new is going to happen to the Jerusalem community. Their audience is the same as it was before, devout Jews who speak Aramaic. Most of the questions that come up are ones that have been answered already.

There is a continued effort to recall everything Jesus said on the many points of discussion. The memories of the Apostles continue to be tapped. But the message is the same, and the audience is familiar with the Law and the Prophets. The answers can be found by searching the sacred texts. The claims about Jesus can be expressed in the traditional, scriptural forms. The group can appear to outsiders so Jewish as to be indistinguishable from traditional believers. Their day still includes Temple worship.

But in Antioch, it is another world. There are many Jewish converts. The first converts among the Gentiles are from the many "God-fearers," people who have become interested in Judaism, and who live according to the Law, and know the sacred texts.

But then pagans start to come forward who want to join the disciples. What do you do with them? The problem is that they are not circumcised. Like all good Jews, the disciples have never worshipped with the uncircumcised. The converts from paganism do not know the proper foods. What do you do at table? The disciples have never eaten foods forbidden by the Torah.

In their preaching, even when they were still in Jerusalem, they had made it clear that Jesus superseded the Law. But they had not changed their own practice of the Law. They continued to circumcise their sons. They continued to avoid forbidden foods. It was one thing to preach Jesus' superiority over the Law to those who lived according to the Law. It is something else when you are preaching to people who have never heard of the Law. Questions arise: what is this Law that has been superseded? Why do we have to pay any attention to it when it has been surpassed? Why should I bother to study and learn a Law that is outdated? Of what use is a Law that considers Jesus' death as a curse?

The logic is clear, but what about at table? How can we eat at the same table if you follow a restricted diet with foods that have been prepared in special ways, and I don't? But if we can't sit at the same table, how can we be brothers and sisters? Something has to give. Someone has to give.

To some of the disciples the answer is obvious: we must all stop following the Torah: we must accept the full logic of our insights about Jesus: we must eat whatever is set before us. These disciples do not want to circumcise the uncircumcised converts. They do not feel bound to teach these converts from paganism the minutiae of Mosaic Law.

To others, such a path is unthinkable. They can no more ignore the dietary laws than they could start practicing sexual promiscuity. This is also forbidden by the Law—is it then to be thrown aside, too? Ridiculous! They want each pagan to become circumcised and instructed in the Torah at the same time that they are baptized. In that way, were they to visit Jerusalem and meet the Apostles, they would be perfectly comfortable, in the Temple, in the synagogue, and at the supper-ritual.

What then is to be preserved, and what can be ignored? Here, in Antioch, the question becomes acute, and there is no clear answer. The Apostles are so far away. What would Jesus have said about it? They need more input from the Apostolic recollections of Jesus' words and spirit. But it is not convenient any more.

Meanwhile back in Jerusalem, the routine goes on from day to day. As the word comes back from Antioch, and the new questions are asked, the congregation is amazed. What unexpected events! What can it mean? The Gentiles are coming in. A memory is stirred. A past moment is recalled. Jesus said something about the pagans walking into God's kingdom and the chosen people standing outside. "Do you remember?"

"Do you remember that afternoon he was so frustrated—in Capernaum. He daydreamed about going to Tyre and preaching there, and how the pagans would listen."

"Then there was the Roman centurion who had more faith than the Apostles themselves!"

So the discussion goes on. But for the Jerusalem Church, it's not a pressing issue. They have no pagans knocking on their door. There is no need to make an immediate decision. There's no one standing there, embodying the problem. It's rather curious but not very urgent. They can afford to spend time wondering: what can it mean? Where is the Spirit in all this? What path is to be followed? What is going on up there in Antioch? Have you heard the latest?

At first, it seems simple: let the pagans learn about the Law and the Temple. Let them be circumcised and become one with us. "What's the problem?" It's only when you have a concrete human being in front of you, and this person does believe in Jesus, but does not know the superseded Law, that you feel how unfair it is to saddle this person with such an unnecessary burden. The Jerusalem Church doesn't have the problem.

Besides, it's not as if it were happening here in Israel. It's just a peripheral event in a place far distant from where the imminent return of Jesus will take place. Who knows what the answer is—it's not of central concern anyway.

They wait and see. There is no doubt at all that something unexpected is happening: Gentiles are becoming disciples.

The conversion of Gentiles is just an odd, unexpected happening with no clear import, a curious development.

But in Antioch, things keep on changing. The disciples do attend the synagogues, but they are known to be different. Their faith in Jesus-Messiah, Jesus the Christ, marks them out. They are called Christians. Saul of Tarsus is transformed into Paul. He arrives and becomes a disciple. He begins to focus his preaching on the Gentiles. He is very reluctant to make the new converts from paganism follow the Mosaic Law. He agrees with those who see clearly that the Law of Moses has no more force. He is a very emotional speaker and a most forceful writer. One of his big advantages is that he knows the Law so well. His Pharisaic background lends authority to his opinions.

The Christian Church in Antioch is changing: pagans are coming in and they are not being circumcised; disciples are eating with them and not worrying about the dietary laws; the converts are enthusiastic in their devotion to Jesus, the Son of God.

In AD 44, the disciples in Jerusalem run into a persecution. Peter and some others leave Jerusalem on missionary journeys. The very conservative James dominates the Church. The practices of the Antioch Church get more and more attention as time passes.

The Christian community of Antioch does not think of itself as independent. They are conscious of being part of the community of disciples led by the Apostles. Stephen had followed that path. They value the prestige of those who had known Jesus in the flesh.

Nor had Stephen's bold preaching been criticized by the Apostles even though it had led to the violent persecution. Stephen's actions were accepted as God's Spirit at work. The claims he had made that had so angered the Jews were not rejected nor even qualified by the Apostles. After all, Stephen was a devout Jew who worshipped in the Temple daily up to the day he had been stoned to death. Stephen had always wanted to walk in step with Peter, James, and John. There had been no friction. No Apostolic eyebrows had been raised.

This sense of being part of one community is the experience of the Antioch Christians also. Repeatedly they bring their questions to Jerusalem. In the year AD 49 Paul himself is in the group that comes to Jerusalem. The issues he raises are not about Jesus and his identity. There is no divergence there. They concern instead the Mosaic Law and the Gentile converts.

The exchanges are typical of the relationships between the two communities. Paul feels free to push his opinion boldly. Peter is pliant, so much so that he seems to be always agreeing with the last person to speak. The leadership is humble. They have vivid memories of their headstrong folly, and they have made those memories available to the believers.

But they also remember how comfortable Jesus was with Temple worship. Despite all the criticism he had voiced, he kept bringing the disciples with him to the Temple Mount for prayer and for preaching.

So Antioch seeks the approval of the Apostolic congregation for what they are doing. The Apostles accept some very radical suggestions and give their blessing. A general agreement is reached, allowing the Antioch Christians much freedom. But the changes are not introduced in Jerusalem.

In the 60s, the Jerusalem Church itself is scattered during the

Great Jewish Revolt. Peter and the disciples cross over completely into the Greek cultural world. This second catastrophe brings about a remarkable clarification of the identity of the Christians. The believers Peter now meets are so far removed from the Galilee of his past. But he can see that their faith in Jesus is just as authentic as his own. It is a strange world, but the Lord is leading them still. Peter is much in demand. He knew Jesus in the flesh. Everything he can remember is precious to the new believers. In addition to the new hymns that are constantly being written, the specific memories of Jesus' life are also becoming a sacred text.

How strange it must have been for Peter. He had been a fisherman, and he had met a young man. Now he was an "authority" on the coming of the end-time for hundreds of people he would never have met. He travels to parts of the world he had never thought of. How attentively they listen as he talks of this spectacular man and his splendid life, and how he had misunderstood Jesus, and resisted him, and finally denied him.

Jesus had promised them so many years before that he would make them "fishers of men." This is what the fishing consisted in: tell the tale of his life and death and resurrection. They will come. People will believe. Fear not! The harvest will be great.

15

Some of the Early Hymns

Hymns were to continue to be crucial throughout the first century of the Church's existence. Those who composed the hymns were the theologians of their day. Because the hymns reached a wide audience, and produced immediate reactions, they were the theological journals of their time. The composers dialogued with one another, supporting or correcting what had gone before.

Here is a typical hymn composed for an early liturgy by John. He had originally been a follower of the Baptist. One evening at the supper he is to preside but first he gets Andrew to introduce this new song. Andrew intones the refrain:

> You are worthy
> because you were killed.

The group learns it quickly. During the liturgy in which John will solo, the rest of the group will be led in for the refrain.

> And with your blood
> you bought people for God
> of every race, language, and nation,
> and made them a line of priests and kings for God,
> to rule the world.
> Worthy is the Lamb that was killed
> to receive power, riches, wisdom,
> strength, honor, glory, blessing.
> To the One seated on the throne and to the Lamb,
> be all praise, honor, glory, and power,
> forever and ever.
> —Cf. Revelation 4:9-10, 12-13

Into the praise of God a second figure is introduced, the Lamb, and the Lamb is offered the same praise that traditionally is reserved for God. Glory is assigned to the Lamb, Jesus, in words that put no ceiling on what might be his true significance, but it is done in traditional terms.

The Lamb's death has made the difference. Through it the world has been transformed and people have become candidates for kingship. The Lamb himself shares the throne of God. At the supper the disciples touch the newly structured heavens. There is a new figure up there, right in the center with God.

Here is another very early hymn. Imagine the disciples at Antioch gathered for supper. The ritual opens with this hymn:

> You are the image of the invisible God,
> first to be born again from the dead.
> You are preeminent in every way
> over all things in heaven and on earth,
> everything seen and unseen,
> thrones, dominations, principalities, powers.
> God wants you to contain all fullness within yourself.
> Through you all is reconciled to God.
> He made peace through the blood of the cross.

Years later it will be quoted in the opening of the Letter to the Colossians (Col.1:15-20).

How far we have come from the messianic psalms. Yet it does not have the carefully crafted technical language of the great christological controversies that would erupt much later. The hymn-composers turn to the only language that can express the world of meaning present in Jesus, the language of poetry. They stretch themselves and they invite their hearers to stretch themselves into an unexplored and imprecise meaningfulness.

Joy is the mood of the early hymns. The death of Jesus is "for us." We are reconciled with God and no other power can change that. Human existence is enveloped in God's spectacular decision to forgive freely.

In the Hebraist community of the Apostles in Jerusalem, the focus always includes the forgiveness of sin. Here is a typical hymn of theirs affirming that forgiveness. In it the composer uses the angels to demonstrate the much loftier status of Jesus.

> You are the radiant image of the glorious God.
> You are the flawless imprint of God's essence.
> By your command you uphold all things.
> You have become the purification of every sin.
> You have taken your seat
> at the right hand of the Majesty on high.
> How mightier than all the angels!
> How more glorious your name!
> To you alone God said:
> 'You are my son.
> Today I have fathered you.'
> —Hebrews 1:3 ff.

Jesus is without parallel, without category. He is being lifted above everything that can be thought of. At the center of all God's action is Jesus. He is not just a messenger but the blinding light that pours out of the core of the Godhead itself.

During these early years Jesus' real identity is like the chambered nautilus, a sea creature that keeps outgrowing its shell. It patiently builds a new one by adding a new chamber to the old one. It then moves into the new one and lives there until that one is outgrown. Then it starts building a larger chamber. The new one is linked to the old chambers forming a spiral.

So the reality of Jesus keeps escaping the cage of words, breaking out of the inadequate verbal formula, and seeks a larger home. Oliver Wendell Holmes described the life-task of the nautilus in his finest poem, "The Chambered Nautilus." In the last stanza he urges that life of unending growth on himself.

> Build thee more stately mansions, O my soul,
> As the swift seasons roll!
> Leave thy low-vaulted past!
> Let each new temple, nobler than the last,
> Shut thee from heaven with a dome more vast,
> Till thou at length art free,
> Leaving thine outgrown shell by life's unresting sea![18]

When we look back at these earliest hymns, we see the first efforts to express the reality of Jesus: how they move forward, linked to the previous efforts, but themselves giving way before a new attempt. Each formula is shattered by the growing awareness of the unlimited significance of the Jesus-Event.

Here are two hymns from later in the first century that exemplify well this function. They were both composed by disciples who are in the following of the Apostle John.

It was the very beginning.
The Word was there,
only the Word and God.
The Word was God—
the Word and God, in the beginning.

Under him, everything that is, became.
Without him, nothing became.

Life was in him,
Life and Light for men.
Now light shines in darkness
but darkness cannot touch it.

The Word was in the world,
and though it existed under him,
it did not know him.
He came to his own people.
They did not welcome him.
Whoever welcomes him,
can become a child of God.
The Word became flesh.
He dwelt among us.
In him we saw the glory of God's only begotten.
From his fullness we receive
one gift after another.
—John 1:1 ff.

The composer introduces a new title for Jesus. There were various texts in the Scriptures where the Word of God was spoken of, but it was in the writings on Wisdom where this composer found the texts that moved him, texts like this from Sirach, where Wisdom is speaking: "From the mouth of the Most High I came forth."

The focus is not on Jesus' earthly life, but on his role in the celestial drama. He is on a level with God himself. Creation and redemption are events which occur between the Word and God. The human story is the overflow of the story of the Word and God. The very entrance into human history of this transcendent figure overshadows his earthly career. The dignity of his person is now at center stage. The deed he performs is reduced to his unparalleled coming onto the human scene.

At some point, some disciples in the circle of John's followers began to talk of Jesus and to preach about him to outsiders without mentioning his public life. It can sound like they are talking about a force rather than a person. He appears to be an emanation of the Godhead and so far beyond human comprehension that he can be spoken of only in symbolic phrases, or philosophic terms.

The song about Jesus as God's word becomes popular and authoritative among the disciples of John. But some feel it is being used and twisted by some of the preachers to support the idea that Jesus was only an emanation of God and not a flesh-and-blood human. An impulse to spiritualize the Jesus-Event is at work, to make his humanity just a cloak he wore. Some feel he is too lofty to have real flesh, real blood.

But the memories of the Apostles are too vivid to let this happen. They remember a real human face, and the touch of a real human hand. They remember a very real human voice. A corrective is called for, and here are the results of this effort, a song that gained a certain prestige of its own, though it never rivaled the widespread use of the first.

It was already there in the very beginning.
Yet we have listened to it.
We have seen it with our own eyes.
We have gazed on it.
Our hands have touched it.

What? That Word who is Life itself.
That is what became visible—Life itself!
We saw it. We witness to it.
We proclaim it to you—the Deathless Life—
that same life that was with the Father
became visible to us.
1 John 1:1 ff.

The writer accepts the phenomenal aspect that is contained in Jesus. The reality within Jesus was already there in the very beginning, or, as the earlier hymn insisted, there even before the creation, when there was only God. That reality defies clarification. It's a phenomenon. It's an "it."

Describing the reality in Jesus as a thing, a phenomenon, rather than in personal terms came out of memories of Jesus' own words. Someone remembered how Jesus had warned that the present generation would be disgraced at the Last Day. The Ninevites would stand up and condemn them. After all, the people of Nineveh had only Jonah, but they had accepted his preaching. But this generation had not responded even though they had "Something greater than Jonah." It is Jesus speaking of himself as a thing, a phenomenon.

The author of the hymn accepts that. Within Jesus is a reality that pre-exists creation and that was there in the very beginning. But—and here is the corrective—"We are speaking of this very human Jesus, the one we heard and touched and saw with our own eyes. That pre-existent phenomenon was wholly present in this man of flesh and blood. No, that's not quite it either. This pre-existent phenomenon had become the man of flesh and blood." And the discussion went on and on, slowly gaining greater and greater clarification.

This was a strange "phenomenon." When the disciple turned to look at it, he found it already gazing at him through a pair of very human eyes. It was a very human will that had made itself felt. He had run into a very possessive person. He had suddenly found that he belonged to someone else. Someone else began treating him as if he had taken him off the shelf and paid for him at the counter, and as if now the disciple belonged to him.

A parallel might be the way babies interact with us. They have no rights—at least, they are not consciously operating on any rights—but they take us over. We become theirs. They adopt us. We yield to this sweet enslavement. The song tells how the baby is "mighty lak' a rose."

Sometimes older children act with the same boldness. They will adopt a teacher or a coach without anybody's say-so. Suddenly you find yourself being treated as their uncle or their grandfather. It is a rare delight.

The young stranger had said, "Come!" and they came. He didn't establish his rights. He just boldly took people over. "Follow me!" and they left their nets. Not everyone. But for those who did he was something else. It took quite a bit of doing even to begin putting him into words.

Each faith has its peculiarities. Christianity is marked by its focus on dogma and certitude. Councils play a large role in its development, and often the main goal of the council-gathering is to make precise the truth about something. This element of Christianity goes back to the very beginnings.

From the very start there is much effort spent on getting it straight. At first, it is the question: what is the precise path of salvation? But very early on that question is seen to be unanswerable without settling another question: who precisely is Jesus?

In this earliest stage, the groups of disciples are small enough to meet together and to interact frequently. In composing their hymns their minds can explore the still unclarified world of meaning that is being experienced in their relationship with Jesus. The pattern of hymn-singing facilitated the rapid development of the answers to questions about the meaning of Jesus.

The earliest disciples found themselves a community focused in on the identity of Jesus of Nazareth. This focus came out of the particularities of the life and teaching of their founder. This swiftly developing focus on the founder's precise dignity, occurring within the first decades of his death, is without parallel in the history of religions. Muhammad and Moses never become confused with God, and Buddha's divine status involved a slow growth over centuries. Christianity is odd in this way. So much so that one of the commentators suggests that Christianity has no revelation, only a revealer.

It has stayed that way. "Who do men say that I am?" The earliest Church can be seen as a community formed to answer that question and to involve others in that effort. It chose so to focus! The ambiguities present in their earliest choices, made without doubts or questions, irresistibly worked their way to the surface of the community's consciousness.

This book has been an effort to project a plausible scenario for that first series of steps by which the band of Galilean "backwoodsmen" carried their concerns into the first-century Empire, despite a language and a culture largely alien to their own.

16

Foundations for a Projection

The Jesus Seminar has made popular the question: "What did Jesus actually say?" It had been a central concern of many Scripture scholars for over a century. The Jesus Seminar threw out a majority of the words put in Jesus' mouth in the four Gospels.

This raises another question: "If Jesus did not actually say these words, then who put them into his mouth?" The obvious answer is: "The Earliest Church." And this raises further questions: "When did they create this new Jesus?" and "Why did they make up all these sayings and attribute them to Jesus?"

Another way of putting the question is: "How did we get the New Testament?" Does it give us a reasonably accurate description of the extraordinary life and teachings of this one person, Jesus of Nazareth, or was it so much the product of the creative imagination of the Christians of the first century that it tells us little about the actual life and teachings of Jesus?

The key to the puzzle then, is the earliest Church. In between the life and death of Jesus and the composition of the writings collected in the New Testament there was the Church. What can we say about the earliest Church? Were there elements in the life of the earliest Church whose presence cannot be easily explained except by a Jesus of Nazareth who was of superhuman stature? Or is the nature of the earliest Church such that the superhuman image of Jesus that we find in The New Testament can be seen as the likely product of the imaginations of the earliest Christians?

Do we need a special event to explain the development of the earliest Church? Do we need a God-in-the-flesh rising from the dead to explain what we see to be the Church of the first century?

Or can we explain all that we see taking place then by the ordinary processes that occur in newly-founded religious sects?

We have a set of writings which reveal a community in existence well before the end of the first century, a community whose cult centered on Jesus of Nazareth. He had died about the year AD 30. This community originated as a sect of a religion whose most distinctive characteristic was its unbending monotheism.

How did believers in the *one* God of Israel, Yahweh, come to venerate in their worship this executed criminal alongside of Yahweh? How did this twofold object of cult come to be?

Perhaps the existence of this community toward the end of the first century is rather easily explained by what commonly occurs in small sects with the passage of time.

Or was the development so sudden that there was not sufficient time for these ordinary forces to go to work, and so it is very reasonable to conclude that something extraordinary must have happened?

This is the question that dominates the story of the early Church. Did the veneration of Jesus take place suddenly? Or did it occur only gradually over a generation or two? What was the actual time span, months or generations?

If we have fifty years to explain the change from strict monotheism to the veneration of Jesus alongside of God, then no extraordinary event may be needed in its origin. But once this time span is reduced to ten years, or five, or less, there is not enough time for the slow processes of the evolution of communities to explain it. The question of time is crucial in explaining the beginnings of Christianity!

Confucius was raised to the altars many centuries after his death. The apotheosis of Gautama Buddha also occurred only after hundreds of years. These are understandable developments. But what of this crucified criminal? Was he actually venerated by strict monotheists within five or ten years of his death? Was he treated as divine within fifteen or twenty years of his execution?

It would be easier if there were a consensus on how soon this offshoot of monotheism began to exalt Jesus. But perhaps the value of consensus has been exaggerated, not just by the Jesus Seminar, but from the very beginnings of modern Scripture study.

In the world of Scripture scholarship, it is very easy to be impressed by the certitude of the statements made. If you stay with one particular school of scholars, you can conclude that anyone who disagrees with their statements is lacking sanity, so cavalierly are dissenting opinions dismissed.

But when you read the work of one of the dissenters, you often find the same certitude, and the same contempt for anyone who disagrees.

This extraordinary level of felt certitude on both sides of a position is a phenomenon that has bedeviled the scene ever since the Enlightenment with its new-found confidence in the powers of human reason. It was during this period that what up to then had been carefully nuanced indications became certitude-producing proofs.

A new pattern of converting people came to the fore: you showed the prospective convert that the proofs for God's existence and the other parts of the creed were so powerful that any doubt about the statement was irrational. The role of the free will was downplayed. Scripture texts were used as parts of syllogisms; certitude about them became the basis of one's act of faith.

When modern criticism entered the scene, it took on the same tendency of exaggerating the degree of certitude in its conclusions. Wherever a consensus developed about a particular opinion, that opinion was clothed with a certitude resembling the irreversible certitudes of papal infallibility.

But scholarly trends are quite changeable. Today one approach holds the field, and twenty years later it is just a footnote. The same evidence can be plausibly interpreted in different ways, and the interpreter's bias will play an unavoidable role. Every historical inquiry is an act of interpretation.

Stephen Wilson studied the efforts of scholars to clarify the relationship between Jesus and Paul and found them filled with "an unwarranted degree of optimism" about the certitude of the conclusions reached.[19] Wilson concedes that all scholars are aware of their inability to make totally objective judgments, but this is often a merely theoretical awareness. It is easily forgotten, and certitude is asserted for what time may reveal to be a thinly based opinion.

Scholars tend to speak as if "the discipline has somehow reached its zenith in their time."[20] Wilson feels that our experience of the last century of biblical scholarship should leave us with one certainty: that there can be no certainty.

Much as it is with the lists that are put out each week in the college football season, to take an everyday example. Last week the coaches reached a consensus that Miami was the best team in the country, and this week they tell us that there are eleven teams better than Miami. Next week the consensus will form around another list. The one thing we can be sure about is that the coaches are not certain which is the best team, if there is such a thing anyway.

If there is very little certitude in matters of historical reconstruction, what value is there in reading the scholars when we try to reconstruct the period of the earliest Church? Why not just spin it out of the unbridled imagination?

If anyone desires to present a reconstruction that has plausibility to it, and that may help another person to a more valid faith decision, then they have to take into account the vast scholarly world that has studied the period carefully. They do not have to accept any particular opinion, no matter how strong is the certitude with which it is expressed, and not even if it is supported by the majority. But they must have some support for their choices.

What then do *some* scholars say about those first years of the early Church? When did the early monotheism of the disciples of Jesus take on a binitarian note with Jesus being reverenced alongside of God?

The sources indicate that the veneration of Jesus occurred quickly. The scholars' writings are filled with phrases like: "From the first few years," "Very close in time to the origin of Christianity," "The most primitive period," "At the earliest stages," "Easily within the first decade." In the first moment "the crucified Jesus had been exalted to a position of heavenly glory."[21] This initial exaltation of Jesus occurred not just in their thinking about him but in cultic worship. The most primitive traditions about Jesus arise from the earliest cultic practices. "There is evidence that the earliest followers of Jesus worshipped Him as their Lord, and accorded Him such divine honours as belonged properly to their covenant God."[22] The supper-ritual was the centerpiece of the life of the earliest Church. In the very beginning the disciples still did not know Jesus, but they did know where they could meet him. The basic everyday experience of Jesus which had been theirs during his public life was continuing in their encounters with him at the suppers.

Like many of the members of the First Continental Congress who were not conscious of the coming of independence, the earliest disciples were not aware of exactly what they were doing at these rituals, but they did feel called to do it. They were not conscious of any incompatibility between the supper and the Temple. They considered the redefinition of their devotion to the God of their fathers "not only as legitimate but, indeed, as something demanded of them."[23] The cultic behavior was not questioned: "Should we be doing this?" When disputes did arise, they did not involve the role that the Risen Lord played in the cult.

Because the cultic suppers played such a significant role, the composition of hymns was to prove of great importance. Right from the earliest years, and throughout the first century of the Church's existence, "the liturgical hymn to Christ was an essential influence on the development of christological thought."[24] In these hymns we can see the earliest reflections on the meaning of Jesus. It is such an unlooked-for phenomenon. Here in the earliest moments of the Christian movement, the writing of hymns is at the cutting edge of theological speculation.

Within the first five years of Jesus' death, a christology was well on its way.[25] Scholars repeatedly stress the extraordinary swiftness of christological development, of the "sudden and significant difference in character from Jewish devotion" occurring at an early stage.[26] "[T]his particular 'chief agent' of this particular Jewish sect quickly became the object of the sort of religious devotion normally reserved for God alone."[27] A binitarian devotion pervaded the earliest Christian groups.[28]

"[I]n a very short time the 'dynamic and creative impulse' of the primal event... laid the foundations for the christology which predominates in the New Testament."[29] "The time between the death of Jesus and the fully developed christology which we find in the earliest Christian documents... is so short that the development... can only be called amazing."[30] "The earliest Christian community created with astonishing speed a christology in which [Jesus] appeared as the fulfiller of the promises of the old covenant, the sole mediator of salvation, indeed as the one fulfiller of God's revelation from the beginning."[31] There isn't the slightest indication that this rapid development in thinking about Jesus was in any way a problem for the Apostles and the Hebraic community. There are sharp differences of opinion among them, but they are never about Jesus.

The scholars are drawn to focus on those first years when Jerusalem was still the world of all the disciples. They search the available data to get some picture of what life was like during this earliest period. Because it is wrapped in much darkness, it lends itself to elaborate hypotheses.

The earliest disciples were devout Jews who shared that fierce devotion to the oneness of God that marked out Jewish history. The disciples would have considered any suggestion of polytheism an abomination. For Jews it was *the* abomination. They were quite familiar with pagan practices and they considered them disgusting. To raise a mere mortal to become the center of cult was a violation of the greatest of the commandments. Only with great effort had Jews been able to get dispensed by the Empire from taking part in the state worship.

That leaves us with the question: how could they have so swiftly made such a drastic change in their devotional life? Could it be that there were pagan influences at work?

> What if as Philip is leaving the temple one day, just a few weeks after the feast of Pentecost, two men come up to him. They ask him many questions about his preaching. They are from Antioch where they run a small shrine dedicated to Hermes. They have come to Jerusalem to visit the shrine of the Jews and they are very disappointed that they are not allowed into the best parts of the temple.
>
> Philip spells out for them the good news of Jesus, the new temple of God, totally accessible to all people: how he had died just a few months before and how he had been raised from the dead. They are hypnotized by Philip's eloquence. After a long day together, Philip agrees to baptize them, for they must leave for Antioch at daybreak.
>
> That evening they attend the supper and Philip explains the meaning of the brief rituals.
>
> When they arrive back in Antioch they begin to win over

many of their friends and relatives. In fact all the members of the governing board of the shrine are baptized in one day, and they start to use the shrine itself for their Jesus ritual. For them, Jesus is the real god come down to earth, and they use many of the rites they had used for Apollo in their new worship. Two years later, after the death of Stephen, some Jerusalem disciples arrive in Antioch. To their delight they find a rather large body of believers active in the city.

In such a scenario it is easy to see how Jesus is quickly given divine status. The pagan converts can't help but elevate Jesus above the gods. They had never seen Jesus, nor are they all that aware of the events of his life. Their concern is the meaning Jesus has in their lives now, and what joy he can bring into the lives of their neighbors. In the process of elevating Jesus into an effective competitor of the other gods, they founded a completely new religion.

There are many scholars who disagree with the plausibility of any such scenario. They see the sources clearly indicating that the veneration of Jesus occurred quickly, and the pagan converts had no influence until long after the earliest christology had already been formed. "The Jewish Christians were always the spiritual driving force which determined the content of the theology." [32] "Before the Apostolic Council [about AD 49] one should not speak of 'Gentile-Christian communities,' but more precisely of 'mixed communities.' The mix in any particular community could change, but at all events the Jewish Christians remained the spiritual and theological leaders."[33] "The mission to the Gentiles apart from the law in the decisive early period is completely and utterly the work of Christian Jews. The consequence is that even in this early period one cannot assume any direct, massive pagan influences."[34]

Another scenario that has been quite popular is to make Paul the major creative genius. Some even hold that his notable lack of interest in the life of Jesus comes from his complete lack of any connection with Jerusalem. They see him as a pure Hellenistic diaspora Jew who was not appreciative of his Jewish background and who knew little of what the Jerusalem Church believed about Jesus. This suggests he easily shook loose from his monotheistic past, and created the image of the divine Jesus.

But Paul's letters contain many fragments of material he had received from the earliest disciples. Much of it is christological, and none of it suggests any tension between him and the Jerusalem Church over the identity of Jesus.

It is not unreasonable to presuppose that Paul's persecution of the disciples "was occasioned partly by the reverence they gave to Jesus."[35] It is not unlikely that many Jews considered the Jesus-devotion of the disciples to violate the uniqueness of God. His conversion was then precisely a call to reverence Jesus and *at the same time* think of himself "as worshipping *one God*."[36] There is little plausibility to the suggestion that Paul transformed a Galilean healer into a divine redeemer. "Paul merely thought through consistently and radically, to the end, the partial criticism of the Torah in a christological and soteriological perspective which had already been introduced by Jesus and was taken further by the Hellenists of Stephen's group (Acts 6.11, 13 f.)."[37] "The real problem for the origin of earliest Christian christology lies in the first four or five years which are 'pre-Pauline' in the full sense of the word." [38] Critical to all the research is the task of uncovering the role of that Hellenist community that had gathered around Stephen. That their intuition about the universal meaning of Jesus' life predates Paul can be seen in the hymn Paul quotes in the second chapter of the Letter to the Philippians. The composition of this hymn goes back to "the very first stratum of Palestinian Christianity."[39] In fact, "In Stephen we have a candidate for the authorship of the hymn. He was a Hellenistic Jewish Christian, of wide sympathies and with depth of penetration into the mystery of Christ. He saw beyond the bounds of a Jewish-Christian mission, to a universal Church."[40]This Hellenist congregation was the "needle's eye" through which the message passed from its Galilean beginnings to the Empire.[41] But its existence is very brief. "The murder of Stephen and the break-up of the Greek-speaking part of the community took place… about AD 32/33."[42]

But if there was no stretch of fifty years, and if there are no pagan influences at work in the first decades, how can such a drastic change be explained?

We are driven back to the originating events. But here you run up against "the modern dogma of the completely unmessianic

Jesus."[43] According to this conviction, Jesus was a merely human reality who soon became the object of a remarkable spate of mythologizing that dominated the evolution of the early Church. But this leaves us with no solution. Hengel puts it succinctly: "As far as I can see, had Jesus not made messianic claims, not only his actions and his fate, but also the rapid development of christology after Easter would be completely incomprehensible."[44] The extraordinary rapidity of christological development is due to the even more extraordinary originating event. Any other approach to the explanation of the development of the earliest Church fails to take into account the impact of the resurrection event: "would it not be possible that the greater part of the roots of later christological development lie in this revolutionary event which radically changed not only Paul's life but also that of Jesus' disciples, that is, in so far as it was not already rooted in the activity and proclamation of Jesus himself?"[45] There is no need to reach for non-existent pagan or gnostic influences on the earliest years of Christianity. These are desperate mythmakings designed to avoid the unparalleled nature of the originating events. To such mythmakers any suggestion seems more plausible than an actual resurrection from the dead.

Hengel contends that the originating events were twofold. There was primarily the messianic nature of Jesus' public life, and the extraordinary impact it had on so many people.

Second, there was the "radical change brought about by the resurrection appearances."[46] Jesus' death as a criminal followed swiftly by his resurrection appearances led to the formation of a community brimming with energy and creativity.

Having seen the risen Jesus, and having become convinced of the dawn of God's kingdom, the disciples left Galilee filled with a deep joy. Hengel quotes Wellhausen's apt phrase: "Enthusiasm gave birth to Christianity."[47] But Hengel insists that it was not just the enthusiasm of the disciples. We must go back to "the eschatological 'enthusiasm' of Jesus, i.e. his unique messianic assurance of God, his awareness that with his activity the kingdom of God was itself dawning."[48] The band of disciples became the continuation of Jesus as he seeks his identity. As it had been with Jesus, the central concern of these early Christians is the salvation of the people. But this salvation is seen more and more as essentially involved in the question of the identity of Jesus himself.

They experience themselves as being inhabited by the same Spirit that had come upon Jesus, and was now being let loose upon the world. Step by step they enter upon the task of articulating the same mystery, a mystery they are entering at each supper-ritual.

Like Jesus they encounter a splendor within him, a splendor that keeps escaping their power to speak it forth: God's great secret, a secret that explains the universe from start to finish. God had a secret son.

The Roman orator Cicero once said that there was only one person in the world who he hoped would surpass him in every way, his son. So too, God had a son, and he wanted that son to be the center of it all. That was the goal God pursued in creating the universe, and in making the sonship available to all. The joy the Father takes in the Son was to be experienced by everyone.

The earliest Church was like a mountain stream. Swelling with new rains, it pours down the mountainside seeking ways of expressing its original conviction. At times, it appears to be satisfied with certain formulae—like the messianic Psalms—but they are only temporary dams behind which the waters keep building up. Soon they begin to pour over the top in their search for better ways to capture that underlying but amorphous and largely inexpressible conviction.

If we lose sight of the conviction that filled the disciples as a result of their experience of Jesus, we are bound to see the more and more grandiose phrases they used of Jesus as wildly creative distortions. But underneath the developing christology was a conviction seeking expression, dissatisfied with all the half-steps, pressing on to the fullness that alone captured the reality they knew to be there.

The early Church served and serves as an arrow pointing to Jesus himself.

Notes

1 Quoted in Martin Hengel, *The Son of God* (Philadelphia: Fortress, 1976), 59.
2 Otto Betz, *What Do We Know About Jesus?* (Philadelphia: Westminster, 1968), 7.
3 Larry Hurtado, *One God, One Lord* (Philadelphia: Fortress, 1988).
4 Hengel, *The Son of God*.
5 Robert Wilken, *Chrysostom and the Jews* (Berkeley: University of California Press, 1983), 75-76.
6 Walt Whitman, "A Noiseless Patient Spider," in *Leaves of Grass* (Philadelphia, David McKay, 1900).
7 Gerard Manley Hopkins, "The Windhover," from *Poems of Gerard Manley Hopkins* (London: Humphrey Milford, 1918).
8 J. A. Fitzmyer, *The Gospel According to Luke* (*Anchor Bible* 28A; Garden City, N.Y.: Doubleday, 1985), 1143.
9 Jessie B. Rittenhouse, ed.,*The Second Book of Modern Verse* (Boston: Houghton Mifflin Company, 1920; New York: Bartleby.com, 2002).
10 Origen, *Contra Celsum* 3:59; tr. Henry Chadwick (Cambridge University Press, 1965), 168.
11 John Bowker, *The Religious Imagination and the Sense of God* (Oxford: Clarendon Press, 1978), 160.
12 H. F. M. (Hilda Frances Margaret) Prescott, *The Man on a Donkey, Part II*, Loyola Reprint Edition (Chicago: Loyola Press, 2010), 542-543. Editor's note: Line breaks are Fr. Sampson's, and not in the original.
13 Thornton Wilder, *Three Plays by Thornton Wilder* (New York: Bantam, 1957), 34.
14 Joseph Cardinal Ratzinger, *Introduction to Christianity* (New York: Herder and Herder, 1970), 192.
15 Ralph P. Martin, *Carmen Christi* (Grand Rapids MI: Eerdmans, 1983) 308.

16 *De vita Mosis*, 1.155.
17 Ibid., 1.158.
18 Oliver Wendell Holmes, "The Chambered Nautilus," *English Poetry III: From Tennyson to Whitman*. Vol. XLII. The Harvard Classics (New York: P.F. Collier & Son, 1909–14; Bartleby.com, 2001).
19 "The Contours and Consequences of a Debate," in *From Jesus to Paul: Studies in Honour of Francis Wright Beare*, ed. P. Richardson and J. Hurd (Waterloo, Ontario: Wilfrid Laurier University Press, 1984), 17.
20 Ibid., 18.
21 Hurtado, *One God, One Lord*, 93.
22 Ralph P. Martin, *Carmen Christi*, 297-298, note 3.
23 Hurtado, *One God*, 11.
24 Hengel, *Between Jesus and Paul*, 89.
25 Ibid., 178, note 76.
26 Hurtado, *One God, One Lord*, 99.
27 Ibid., 117.
28 Cf. Ibid., 115.
29 Hengel, *Between*, 46.
30 Ibid., 31.
31 Hengel, *The Son of God*, 91.
32 Ibid., 67.
33 Hengel, *Between*, 37-38.
34 Ibid., 41.
35 Hurtado, 2.
36 Ibid., 2.
37 Hengel, *Son*, 67-68, note 123.
38 Hengel, *Between*, 44.
39 Hurtado, *One*, 161, note 10.
40 Martin, *Carmen*, 304.
41 Hengel, *Between*, 27.
42 Ibid., 42.
43 Ibid.,33.
44 Ibid., 178-179, note 76.
45 Ibid., 33.
46 Ibid., 44.
47 Ibid., xii, quoting Julius Wellhausen, *Einleitung in die ersten drei Evangelien* (1911), 150.
48 Ibid., xii.

CPSIA information can be obtained
at www.ICGtesting.com
Printed in the USA
FFOW05n1905210216

9 780996 648462